"Greg Laurie is not only a personal friend, but is one of the great communicators of the gospel of Jesus Christ in our generation. I highly recommend him."

BILLY GRAHAM

BECAUSE...

GREG LAURIE

Multnomah® Publishers *Colorado Springs, Colorado*

BECAUSE...
published by Multnomah Publishers
A division of Random House Inc.

© 2006 by Greg Laurie
International Standard Book Number: 1-59052-797-6

Multnomah is a trademark of Multnomah Publishers,
and is registered in the U.S. Patent and Trademark Office.
The colophon is a trademark of Multnomah Publishers.

Printed in the United States of America

For information:
MULTNOMAH PUBLISHERS
12265 Oracle Boulevard, Suite 200
Colorado Springs, CO 80921

06 07 08 09 10 11—10 9 8 7 6 5 4 3 2 1 0

Now when they saw the boldness of Peter and John,
and perceived that they were uneducated and untrained men,
they marveled. And they realized that they had been with Jesus.

ACTS 4:13

GETTING STARTED

We live in an instant-gratification, fast-track, I-want-results-*now* world. Many Christians fall into this trap and seek spiritual growth overnight, looking for a shortcut to getting closer to God.

After a number of years of walking with the Lord and being in ministry, I've discovered *there is no fast track.* In fact, the very opposite is true. The Bible tells us things like "Be still" and "Wait upon the Lord," and it talks about slowing down and exercising discipline as the only true way to deepen our spiritual walk.

This book will help you do just that. It will encourage and challenge you with daily insights into God's Word while you slow down long enough each day to spend time drawing closer to God.

A Test

The truth is that if we want to grow spiritually, we must sink our roots deeply into Jesus Christ. It's a process that the Bible calls *abiding.* "Abide in Me," Jesus commanded us (John 15:4). And for the person willing to do that, He promises a fruitful, spiritually productive life — "I chose you and appointed you that you should go and bear fruit, and that your fruit should remain" (John 15:16).

So let me ask you: What do people see in your life right now?

To help you answer that, take this short test with me:

Do others see…
    love or hatred?
    joy or gloom?
    peace or turmoil?
    gentleness or harshness?
    faith or worry?
    meekness or pride?
    a person of self-control or a victim of worldly passions?

How did you do? Pretty eye-opening isn't it?

If you've been looking for a shortcut to spirituality, then I want to challenge you to use this book for helping you get back to the everyday work of drawing closer to God, bearing fruit, and living out your faith.

Yes, it takes time—and lots of it. But what better way to spend your life than seeking to become more like Jesus as you glorify Him and bring forth spiritual fruit.

The Setup

As you dive in day by day, here's what you can do with each of the daily readings in this book:

1. After getting alone and quiet and still, read my brief comments that start each day's selection.

2. Think over the "sidebar" Scriptures or questions that you'll see in bold type.

3. Ponder carefully the Bible verse under the heading "The Lord's promise to His people." Ask yourself, "What does this mean for *my* life?"

4. Pray. There's no need for any elaborate or religious-sounding words; just talk honestly with God. (You can use the guidelines you'll see under the heading "With God in prayer.") Focus especially on having a grateful heart, and expressing your sincere gratitude to God. (There will *always* be something new each day to thank Him for!)

5. As you continue in prayerful thought, consider the suggestions you'll find under the heading that starts with the word "Because…" (The rest of the heading is different each day.) This suggestion will always relate to actually *doing* something about what God says. Take seriously the fact that God wants you to be "not a forgetful hearer but a *doer*" of His Word — and be excited about His promise that whoever does this "will be *blessed* in what he does" (James 1:23-25).

6. As God's Holy Spirit brings to mind further reflections, application points, and things to pray about, feel free to write these down in the space provided at the end of the daily reading. If you get in the habit of writing something down here each day, this book will become a powerful record of your spiritual journey during this season in your life,

and it will always be a great personal encouragement to come back and
review what God has done.

You'll find enough daily readings here to hast you an entire half-year,
with readings for each weekday plus one for the weekend.

My hope is that as make your way through this devotional readings,
you'll keep asking the Lord to show you how He wants to change your
life day by day. My prayer for you is that the Holy Spirit will shine His
powerful light into your heart, showing you any area that should be
dealt with, and filling you with hope and encouragement for a lifelong
adventure of following the Lord.

APPOINTMENT WITH GOD

Ever had an appointment with someone, say for lunch, and they called and canceled at the last minute? Or worse, they just didn't show?

Adam had an appointment with God every day in the Garden of Eden. He would hear the Lord's voice in the garden in the cool of the evening. But one day Adam missed that appointment because of sin.

So God said to Adam, "Where are you?" (Genesis 3:9).

I wonder if the Lord would say the same thing to some of us many times: "Where are you? Where have you been? I have been looking for you. I wanted to speak with you. I want you to walk with Me—and I want to walk with you." I wonder just how many times each day God wants to tell us something, but He can't get a word in edgewise?

There was the sound of a **gentle** whisper.

1 Kings 19:12 NLT

The Lord might say, "I've wanted to speak to you for a long time, but you're too busy. This morning I wanted to talk to you, but you didn't have any time for Me. You read the newspaper and watched TV and talked on the phone. You never opened My Word. You never prayed."

Reflect on the fact that Almighty God wants to spend **time** with you and **speak** with you. What does that say about His love for you and and His desire to cultivate **friendship** with you?

He might say, "At lunch I tried to say something, but your prayer was so quick. In the afternoon I tried again. But you're always so busy.

"You have an appointment with Me. Why don't you keep it?"

Just imagine: The Creator of the universe wants to spend time with you. *He* wants to meet with *you* on a regular basis! Is there any appointment more worth keeping than this one?

Why make room in your busy schedule for regular time alone with God? Because He has so much to tell you.

> The Lord's promise to His people...
>
> I will meet with you, and I will speak with you.
> EXODUS 25:22

With God in prayer...

Talk to the Lord about your desire to hear from Him. Thank Him for His own longing to meet with you, and for all that this means about His heart of love.

Because He wants to be with you...

Before God, make a solid commitment to spend daily time with Him. Ask someone else (your spouse or a friend) to help keep you accountable to this commitment.

Your own reflections... personal application... personal prayer points...

Tuesday

IN SYNC WITH GOD

I have a German shepherd that was a former guide dog for the blind. Because he developed a slight infirmity in his hip (a common problem with German shepherds), he was put up for adoption. When we got him, he was perfectly trained. We could take him anywhere. He was happy to sit next to us. If another dog walked by, he could care less.

But then I began to unleash him and let him run around in the park. Day by day, he seemed to lose more and more discipline. The next thing I knew, he was lunging at other dogs. He was chasing rabbits all the time. I phoned the people we got him from and asked what went wrong.

Can two people walk together without agreeing on the direction?

Amos 3:3 NLT

They told me I couldn't let him do all that "dog stuff." I couldn't let him stop and sniff wherever he wanted to sniff. I couldn't let him chase rabbits. They gave me a little muzzle-like device to put on him, which would make it hurt for him to pull away. Keeping control of his muzzle meant that I could teach him again to obey. Sure enough, after I used the device for a while, he was in sync with me again.

We can be like that with God. We run around, being crazy, doing whatever *we* want to do. So the Lord has to pull us back into line.

Think about your relationship with the Lord. In what specific ways do you tend to be like a dog that wants to escape its master's control?

Sheep, like dogs, have this same tendency to stray. The Bible says, "All of us have strayed away like sheep. We have left God's paths to follow our own" (Isaiah 53:6 NLT). But God wants us to walk with Him, and to walk with God means I must get into harmony with Him. I must go the direction God wants me to go.

How about you? Are you *walking with God* today?

Or are you pulling against Him, trying to do things your own way? If so, then it's time to stop, ask God's forgiveness, and get in sync with Him once again.

Why go God's way instead of your own? Because "All the ways of the LORD are loving and faithful for those who keep the demands of his covenant" (Psalm 25:10 ESV).

The Lord's promise to His people...

He leads the humble in what is right, teaching them his way.
PSALM 25:9 NLT

With God in prayer...

Ask God to help you better understand your own tendency to get away from His control and direction.

Because He wants to guide you...

Think of just *one situation* in the coming day in which it will likely be easy for you to ignore God's direction. Plan ahead for a way to remind yourself of this weakness when the time comes, and to depend on God's help to stay in harmony with Him.

Your own reflections... personal application... personal prayer points...

Wednesday

A HEART UNDIVIDED

The apostle Paul once said, "I am focusing all my energies *on this one thing:* Forgetting the past and looking forward to what lies ahead" (Philippians 3:13 NLT).

Now there's someone with an undivided heart! Many of us today could say, "I focus all my energies on these eight things" or "on these four things"—instead of "on this *one* thing." It's the problem of a divided heart.

I run straight to the goal with purpose in every step.
1 Corinthians 9:26 NLT

You know...what my purpose in life is.
2 Timothy 3:10 NLT

When Jesus said, "Blessed are the pure in heart," that word *pure* means "undivided." In other words, blessed (or happy) is the man or woman with an undivided heart. Happy is the person who knows where he or she is going in life, who has priorities and lives by them. Happy is the person who isn't trying to live in two worlds.

We live in such a wicked time, and we're exposed to so many things that can be spiritually harmful. It seems that today we so often lack "purity"—"undividedness." But according to Romans 16:19, as believers we're "to be wise as to what is good and innocent as to what is evil" (ESV). Another version expresses it as being "well versed and wise as to what is good" while also being "innocent and guileless as to what is evil" (AMP).

Reflect on this question: Is it correct to say that whatever we spend the most energy on in our life is our true highest purpose?

God is offering you true happiness, and it isn't contingent on how much you have, but on *who you know*. What better reason can you think of for getting to know God better? If you do, and if you get your life properly aligned with Him, you'll never be chasing elusive dreams. If you keep seeking Him, you *will* find purpose in life. And by finding it, you'll discover the happiness you deeply crave.

The Lord's promise to His people...

Happy are those who are strong in the LORD.
PSALM 84:5 NLT

With God in prayer...

Ask God to make clear to you your purpose in this life.

Because He blesses a pure heart...

Right now, write down your God-given purpose in life, to the best of your understanding.

Your own reflections... personal application... personal prayer points...

Thursday

LOVE IS THE REASON

A lot of Christians think they should keep the Ten Commandments because they're afraid God will punish them if they don't. But a truer perspective is that God loves us, and we're therefore to keep His commandments *out of awareness of this love.*

We need to know that God accepts us as we are. By His grace, "He made us accepted in the Beloved"—in Jesus Christ (Ephesians 1:6). We don't have to do anything to earn His approval. We don't have to do anything to merit His love. In spite of our shortcomings, in spite of our sins, *God loves us.*

What comes to your mind when you reflect on the word **father**? Is it valid as a picture of God's love?

Some people come from homes in which their fathers never expressed love to them or showed them any affection. And they take this distorted concept of an earthly father and place it on their heavenly Father. They spend the rest of their life trying to earn God's approval—when in fact He has already given them that approval. He loves us as we are. Of course, He doesn't want to leave us that way. He wants to change us so we become more like Christ. Even then, it remains true that God loves us no less when we fail than He does when we do well.

Do you **love** Me?
Jesus, in John 21:17

Realizing this should cause us to *want* to love Him. As 1 John 4:19 says, "We love Him because He first loved us." So instead of wanting to keep God's commandments to earn His love, we should want to keep them *because of* His love for us. We should want to keep His commandments because we know they're right, and that keeping them will please the One we most want to please.

It all comes down to our motives.

> The Lord's promise to His people...
>
> Nothing in all creation will ever be able to separate us from the love of God that is revealed in Christ Jesus our Lord.
> ROMANS 8:39 NLT

With God in prayer...

Ask the Lord to be at work today to strengthen your loving motives for obeying Him.

Because He's your loving Father...

In the coming day, what's the most important action you can take to demonstrate your genuine love for your Father in heaven?

Your own reflections... personal application... personal prayer points...

Friday

OUR HABIT OF WANDERING

When my son was little, he had a habit of wandering.

One day we were in a hotel and approached an elevator. He ran ahead to push the button. I told him, "If the elevator comes, wait until Dad gets there before you go in." But just as I arrived at the elevator, the doors were closing—with my son inside. He was gone. I frantically pushed the button for the other elevator and waited for what seemed an eternity. Finally the doors opened, and I jumped in.

I went down to the lobby. He wasn't there. I ran back to the elevator and pushed every button for every floor. As the doors opened I would scream out his name. I didn't care about decorum; I wanted to find my son.

In your life, can you remember any "elevator rides" you've taken alone, when you wish you had waited for God?

I found him about three floors up, wandering around. But you know what? After that experience, he didn't wander anymore. He'd been separated from his dad, and it was scary for him. He learned how important it was to stay close to me.

As Christians, we should want to stay as close to our heavenly Father as possible. I have a healthy respect for the devil's ability; he's a powerful adversary. In our own strength, we're no match for him. So we don't want to venture out in this life depending only on our own abilities, because it will bring spiritual defeat.

Be strong in the Lord and in the power of His might.
Ephesians 6:10

It is good for me to draw **near** to God.

Psalm 73:28

That's why I want to stay as close to the Lord as possible. I want to be strong in Him.

If ever there was a time to be walking closely with the Lord, it's now. This is not the time to be playing games with God. This is not the time to wander away.

The Lord's promise to His people...

Draw near to God and He will draw near to you.

JAMES 4:8

With God in prayer...

Talk honestly with the Lord about how much you want to stay close to Him in your life *today*.

Because of your tendency to wander...

Sometime in the next twenty-four hours, there's at least one "elevator door" that will open and invite you inside, *alone*—without God. Imagine yourself there—and make the decision *now* not to step inside without Him.

Your own reflections... personal application... personal prayer points...

TRUE FRIEND

Sometimes the best thing you can do for a hurting person is to just be there.

When I was a young pastor, I had a three-point sermon for just about everyone. But since then, I've often stood with people who have experienced a tragedy or loss, and I realized they didn't necessarily need a sermon. Often what they need is just a friend. They don't need someone to say, "I know what you're going through," or "Maybe this is the reason for it." They need someone to just love them, pray for them, and cry with them because of the great sense of loss they're experiencing.

> He said to them, "My soul is exceedingly sorrowful, even to death. Stay here and watch with Me."
>
> Matthew 26:38

Jesus experienced loneliness. He experienced anguish. In the Garden of Gethsemane, He asked Peter, James, and John to stay with Him. But only a short while later, when authorities came to arrest Him, "all the disciples forsook Him and fled" (Matthew 26:56).

And then, in the loneliest moment of His life, He cried out from the cross, "My God, My God, why have You forsaken Me?" (Matthew 27:46). It's believed by many (myself included) that at this very moment, God poured upon His sinless Son the punishment for all the sin of all of humanity. The heavenly Father, who is holy, turned His face from His Son. Jesus was momentarily separated from Him. And in that moment, Jesus experienced a loneliness totally beyond anything we've ever known.

Think about the loneliness you've known, and compare it to what you know about the loneliness Jesus experienced. How were they alike?

So the next time you're feeling down, the next time you're feeling misunderstood, the next time your friends seem to have forsaken you, be assured that you can go to Jesus for the comfort and encouragement you need. Why? Because *Jesus has been there.* He knows what it's like. And He'll never leave you or forsake you in your hour of pain.

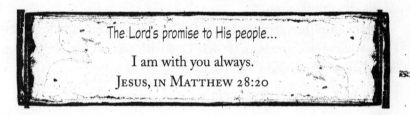

The Lord's promise to His people...

I am with you always.
JESUS, IN MATTHEW 28:20

With God in prayer...

Give thanks to Jesus for the loneliness He went through for our sake.

Because He knows all about loneliness...

Not far away from you, there's someone struggling with loneliness. Think about who that might be. When will you go and spend time with that person?

Your own reflections... personal application... personal prayer points...

GOD WITH SKIN

I heard the story of a little boy who was frightened one night during a thunderstorm. He called out from his room, "Daddy, I'm scared!"

His father, not wanting to get out of bed, called back, "Don't worry, Son. God loves you and will take care of you."

There was a moment of silence. Then the little boy's sounded again from his room. "Daddy, I know God loves me, but right now I need somebody with skin on."

Sometimes, our great and awesome God seems almost untouchable. That's where Jesus comes in. He was God with skin on, walking among us and showing us what God is like.

> So the **Word** became human and lived here on earth among us.
>
> John 1:14 NLT

> He will be called **Immanuel** (meaning, God is with us).
>
> Matthew 1:23 NLT

C. S. Lewis put it well: "The Son of God became a man that men might become sons of God."

God became a human being so that you might become God's child. But no one begins life this way, as a child of God; the Bible says that we must be born again (John 3:3). There must come a moment in our life when we turn from our sins and invite Jesus Christ to come in and take over our life as Savior and Lord.

Have you done that yet? The choice is yours.

And if you *have* chosen Jesus, you can know with certainty that if you die today, you'll go to heaven, and live with Him forever.

The Lord's promise to His people...

To all who believed him [Jesus Christ] and accepted him, he gave the right to become children of God.

JOHN 1:12 NLT

With God in prayer...

Give specific thanks to the Lord Jesus for coming to this earth and walking among us, and then dying on the cross to purchase our salvation.

Because He saved you...

Thankfulness for your eternal salvation is the key to joy in daily life. What can you do to help remind yourself of what Jesus has done for you?

Your own reflections... personal application... personal prayer points...

READ THE MANUAL

If you want to learn about Jesus, learn to study this wonderful book God has given us, the Bible. It's the user's manual of life. It tells us what is right and wrong and what is good and evil. It tells us how to live, how to relate best with others, how to do business, how to have a fulfilling marriage and family.

But most importantly, the Bible tells us how to know and walk with God. In fact, everything you need to know about God is found in the pages of your Bible.

> I have come to do your will, O God—just as it is written about me in the Scriptures.
>
> Hebrews 10:7 NLT

Abraham Lincoln said of the Bible, "All of the good from the Savior is communicated through this Book. All things that are desirable to man are contained in it."

Sadly, many people today own Bibles but seldom read them. As many as 93 percent of Americans own at least one Bible, but surveys indicate that little more than half read it, and far fewer read it every day.

Yet success or failure in the Christian life is determined by how much of the Bible you get into your heart and mind on a daily basis and how obedient you are to what you read. Think about that for a moment.

In what ways exactly has the Bible already shaped your own heart and mind?

What amazes me are Christians who have known the Lord for many years, yet don't read the Bible. They attend church and Bible studies, they listen to Bible teaching a little here and a little there, but they don't habitually open the Word of God and read it for themselves.

If you want to grow spiritually, this must become a regular part of your life. It's essential. And the need for it is something you'll never outgrow, any more than you'll ever outgrow your need for eating or breathing.

· The Lord's promise to His people...

If you abide in My word [hold fast to My teachings and live in accordance with them], you are truly My disciples. And you will know the Truth, and the Truth will set you free

JESUS, IN JOHN 8:31-32 AMP ·

With God in prayer...

Express your gratitude to God for specific ways that He has spoken to you and helped you through His Word, the Bible.

Because His Word is your life...

Evaluate your normal daily routine. Do you need to make any changes to help you guard and maintain a daily time with God in reading the Bible and praying?

Your own reflections... personal application... personal prayer points...

Wednesday

JUST PRAY

Three pastors were debating the best posture for prayer. One claimed the best way to pray is to always have your hands pressed together and pointing upward. The second insisted the best way to pray is on your knees. The third was convinced the best way to pray is stretched out on the floor, flat on your face.

As they were debating, a repairman from the telephone company overheard their conversation while he was working in the next room. He walked in and said, "Excuse me, gentlemen. I don't mean to interrupt, and I'm certainly no theologian. But I've found that the most powerful prayer I've ever prayed was when I was dangling upside down from a power pole, suspended forty feet above the ground."

When we truly recognize our need, prayer becomes real.

> They cried out to the LORD in their trouble,
> and He saved them out of their distresses.
>
> Psalm 107:13

And when we look at instances of prayer in the Bible, we discover that any posture will do. People prayed while standing, lifting their hands, sitting, lying down, kneeling, lifting their eyes, bowing, and even pounding their chest.

We also see that any place will do. People prayed on a battlefield, in a cave, in a closet, in a garden, on a mountainside, by a river, on the sea, in the street, in a home, in bed, in a prison, in the wilderness, and even in the belly of a huge fish. So any place will do.

Last, we find that any time will do. People prayed early in the morning, in the midmorning, in the evening, three times a day, before meals, after meals, at bedtime, and at midnight. Anytime day or night is a good time for prayer.

Listen to my **voice** in the morning, LORD.
Each morning I bring my **requests** to you and wait expectantly.
Psalm 5:3 NLT

Isn't that great to know? You can pray whenever, wherever, however. So just pray.

The Lord's promise to His people...

Call to Me, and I will answer you,
and show you great and mighty things.
JEREMIAH 33:3

With God in prayer...

Bring your praise and needs before God today in prayer.

Because God answers prayer...

What are your greatest needs today, the things you most need to pray about? Make sure to bring these requests to your Father in heaven.

Your own reflections... personal application... personal prayer points...

Thursday

WHERE IS HAPPINESS?

Two strangers riding a commuter train happened to strike up a conversation. One of them seemed distraught and miserable, overcome by troubles.

Seeing his unhappy condition, the other man told him, "Here's an idea for you." He mentioned a famous comedian who was appearing at a nightclub downtown. "I hear he puts everyone in stitches. Go listen to him tonight, and you'll forget how miserable you feel."

After a moment of silence, the first man admitted, "I *am* that comedian."

What is happiness? I think the world's version of it is quite different than the Bible's version. The happiness of this world depends largely on circumstances. If you're in good health, the bills are paid, and things are going reasonably well, then you're happy according to the world's philosophy. But if someone cuts you off on the freeway or you get sick or you incur an unplanned major expense, suddenly you're unhappy. Your happiness always hinges on the given circumstances of the moment.

What usually brings you the most happiness?

The Bible gives us a completely different view of this thing called happiness. According to Scripture, true happiness is never something to be sought directly; it always results from seeking something else.

Happy indeed are those whose God is the LORD.
Psalm 144:15 NLT

BECAUSE . . .

When we're trying to be happy, when we're trying to be fulfilled, we rarely are. But when we forget about those things and get back to the purpose for which God put us on the earth, suddenly we find a wonderful byproduct—happiness—popping up in our lives.

When we seek holiness, we'll find happiness. When we seek righteousness, we'll become happy people, because our will is aligned with the will of God as we walk in harmony with Him. The rest of our lives will then find their proper balance.

> The Lord's promise to His people...
>
> The blessing of the LORD makes one rich,
> and He adds no sorrow with it.
> PROVERBS 10:22

With God in prayer...

Discuss with the Lord any ways in which you may be trying to find happiness apart from Him.

Because God's blessing is true happiness...

What specific actions can you take today in seeking holiness and righteousness (instead of your own happiness)?

Your own reflections... personal application... personal prayer points...

Friday

MOVING FORWARD

A sign along a road at the end of an airport runway reads this way: "Keep moving. If you stop, you endanger yourself and those who are flying."

We could apply the same principle to the Christian life: *Keep moving,* because if you stop, you're in danger.

What exactly is the danger if we stop moving forward and growing? The danger is that we have a natural tendency (our "old nature") to slip back into our former sinful ways. Just as a car going uphill will naturally roll backward if it's parked and shifted into neutral, we'll naturally go the wrong way if we shift our Christian lives into neutral and stop seeking to learn and grow as believers as we develop our "new nature."

> You, dear friends, must continue to build your lives on the foundation of your holy faith.
> Jude 1:20 NLT

Take a flower and a weed, for example. My wife Cathe loves to grow flowers. She'll tend them, care for them, fertilize them, and watch them mature, slowly but surely.

Meanwhile, in the time it takes for those flowers to grow a few inches, a weed can find a crack in the sidewalk and shoot up several feet tall, with no nurture or help whatsoever. It simply takes off.

Our new nature is like a flower, and it needs careful nurturing. We need to do the things that build us up spiritually. If we cease to do those things, our old nature will come back to haunt us. Because our old nature—that part of us that doesn't want to obey God—is like a weed.

BECAUSE . . . .

What is your strongest **motivation** for wanting to grow spiritually?

BECAUSE...

31

And remember, growth in the Christian life isn't just about obeying commandments. It's about *wanting* to grow, *wanting* to please the Lord, and *wanting* to become more like Him. That's what keeps us moving. As the saying goes, whoever ceases to be better, will soon cease to be good.

The Lord's promise to His people...

Then we will no longer be like children....
Instead, we will hold to the truth in love,
becoming more and more in every way like Christ.
EPHESIANS 4:14–15 NLT

With God in prayer...

Talk with God about what "moving forward" spiritually should mean for you right now.

Because God will lead you...

What specific step forward can you make in your spiritual life today?

Your own reflections... personal application... personal prayer points...

WHAT REALLY MATTERS

Over the years, I've done a lot of funerals and memorial services. I've visited people who were literally at death's door, and I can tell you that when your life comes to an end, three things will really matter to you: faith, family, and friends.

Of number one importance will be your faith, your relationship with God. I've heard more people say with regret, "I wish I'd spent more time walking closely with God. I wish I'd made more time for spiritual things." They recognize the fact that very soon they'll be standing before God Almighty. How sad it is when people realize they've squandered their lives.

> Thus says the LORD: "Set your house in order,
> for you shall die, and not live."
> 2 Kings 20:1

Next of importance is your family. "I wish I'd been a better father," some confess at their life's end, or, "I wish I'd been a better mother." Their concern is not about how much money they made, whether they spent enough time at the office, or whether they had plenty of possessions and "toys." They know they're leaving all that behind.

And then friends. And that includes all those outside our family who we've been able to serve and help and love. Relationships are what life is all about.

What truly matters most in your life?

Sadly, however, we spend so much time on that which doesn't really matter in the long run, while we neglect what really does matter—faith, family, friends.

With those things in mind, we want to make sure our lives are always right before God. When King Hezekiah was close to death, the prophet Isaiah told him, "Set your house in order" (2 Kings 20:1). Is your house in order today?

The Lord's promise to His people...

For we must all stand before Christ to be judged.
We will each receive whatever we deserve for the
good or evil we have done in our bodies.
2 CORINTHIANS 5:10 NLT

With God in prayer...

Talk with God about your commitments to your faith, your family, and your friends.

Because your life on earth will come to an end...

Is there anything in your life that you're giving time and energy to, and yet it doesn't really matter eternally? Do you need to make a change in this area to reflect true eternal priorities?

Your own reflections... personal application... personal prayer points...

Monday

YOU'LL GET THERE

There's an interesting story in the Gospels of a time when Jesus invited the disciples—some of whom were seasoned fishermen—to join Him on a boat trip across the Sea of Galilee. On their way over, they encountered a dreadful storm.

Did Jesus know this storm was coming? My answer is yes. In fact, we might even say the storm was a part of His curriculum for His disciples that day. It was all part of teaching them to believe what they claimed to believe.

> He **commands** and raises the stormy wind, which lifts up the waves of the sea.... He **calms** the storm, so that its waves are still.
> Psalm 107:25, 29

We don't want to make light of what these disciples were facing, because I'm sure this was an unusually severe storm. Many of them had certainly experienced major squalls on the Sea of Galilee before, but this one gripped them with fear. As the boat took on water, "they were in real danger," so that they cried out, "we're going to drown!" (Luke 8:23–24 NLT).

What **fears**, if any, are you facing now?

But the disciples didn't have to be afraid. They apparently had forgotten a significant statement Jesus made earlier: "Let us cross over to the other side of the lake" (8:22). And when God says, "We're going to the other side," it means you're going to the other side. That doesn't necessarily mean smooth sailing. It doesn't guarantee an easy trip. But it does mean you'll get there.

Where has God **promised** to take you?

Often we're gripped by fear and we stop thinking logically when we forget God's Word to us. That's exactly what happened to the disciples. But Jesus was on board with them, and He was there to see them through.

The Lord's promise to His people...

Be sure of this: I am with you always.
JESUS, IN MATTHEW 28:20 NLT

With God in prayer...

Talk with God about your life's journey and destination. Where is He taking you?

Because He's with you...

What fear or anxiety do you need to deal with now, as you go forward into the future God has for you?

Your own reflections... personal application... personal prayer points...

Tuesday

DON'T RUN FROM THE CROSS

Have you noticed you don't always know as much as you think you do?

I find I often need certain reminders, because I forget what I ought to remember as a Christian, and I remember what I ought to forget.

In Luke 24 we find the story of two men who had forgotten something they should have remembered. At one time, they'd been passionate followers of Christ, but now their dreams had been destroyed as they watched Him die on a Roman cross.

Earlier, during His ministry with them, Jesus told them He would be crucified, then rise from the dead after three days. He spoke of this often.

> Now behold, two of them were traveling that same day to a village called Emmaus, which was seven miles from Jerusalem. And they talked together of all these things which had happened.
>
> Luke 24:13-14

But they had forgotten, and their hopes about Jesus were fading.

As they admitted to a traveler who joined them on the road from Jerusalem to Emmaus, "The chief priests and our rulers delivered Him to be condemned to death, and crucified Him. But we were hoping that it was He who was going to redeem Israel" (Luke 24:20–21).

Even as Jesus hung on the cross, they hoped for a last-minute miracle. But no miracle came. They felt discouraged. Let down. And they decided to leave town. They wanted to put as much distance between them and the cross as possible.

We need to remember that every step away from the cross is a step in the wrong direction. When we're hurting or have failed spiritually, that isn't the time to run away from the cross. That's the time to run *to* it.

Maybe something has happened to you and you feel as though God let you down. Maybe some tragedy has occurred. But God hasn't failed you. He hasn't forgotten you. Now is the time to run back to the cross.

It wasn't that Jesus had let these men down; rather, they had misunderstood His purpose in coming to begins with. He hadn't come to establish an earthly kingdom then and there. He came to die for their sins (and ours) and then to rise again from the grave.

So when hardship hits, don't run from the cross; run *to* it. Now is the time to remember His Word and the promises it holds for you.

> The Lord's promise to His people...
>
> He who did not spare His own Son, but delivered Him up for us all, how shall He not with Him also freely give us all things?
> ROMANS 8:32

With God in prayer...

Do you sense in any way that the Lord has let you down? Confess this to Him. Like the disciples in Luke 24, you have misunderstood Him.

Because the cross proves His love for you...

What disappointment do you need to let go of? What can you do to help you let go of it, and move forward?

Your own reflections... personal application... personal prayer points...

Wednesday

FAILURE AND SUCCESS

Jesus had risen from the dead. He had appeared to some of the disciples. But there were no clear marching orders, so they thought they would go back to what they knew how to do—fish.

> Simon Peter said, "I'm going fishing."
> "We'll come, too," they all said.
> So they went out in the boat, but they caught nothing all night. (John 21:3 NLT)

After they fished through the night on the Sea of Galilee without catching anything, the morning light revealed the figure of someone standing on the shore. The man called out, "Friends, have you caught any fish?" (John 21:5 NLT). Only later would they realize this was Jesus.

Throughout the Bible, God often asks probing questions when He wants a confession from someone. In the same way, Jesus was asking His disciples, "Have you been successful? Have things gone the way you'd hoped they would go? Are you satisfied?" They had to admit their failure.

Why did Jesus want them to admit this? So He could bring them to something better.

Are you experiencing any failure in your life at this time?

Jesus told them to cast their net again. As they followed His specific instructions, their net became so heavy with fish they couldn't pull it in. The Lord was teaching the disciples an important lesson: Failure often can be the doorway to real success.

We need to come to this point in our lives as well. We need to come to Him and say, "Lord, I'm not satisfied with the way my life is going. I'm tired of doing it my way. I want to do it Your way."

If you'll come to God like that, He'll extend His mercy and grace to you. He'll take your life and transform it in ways you couldn't imagine.

The Lord's promise to His people...

Fear not, for I am with you; Be not dismayed,
for I am your God. I will strengthen you, yes,
I will help you, I will uphold you with My righteous right hand.
ISAIAH 41:10

With God in prayer...

Admit to God any failure you're now experiencing. Be honest with Him and with yourself about this.

Because God is leading you into something better...

What failure do you need to leave behind you?

Your own reflections... personal application... personal prayer points...

Thursday

PROVING YOUR LOVE

Have you ever felt like a spiritual failure? If so, you're in good company. Even the apostle Peter felt that way after he denied the Lord.

When Jesus told the disciples they would abandon Him in His hour of need, Peter insisted *he* never would. But Jesus said Peter would deny Him three times before the rooster crowed. And Peter did just that.

Later, Peter found himself in an awkward moment as he and some of the other disciples encountered the risen Jesus on the shore of the Sea of Galilee. Before they knew it, Jesus was cooking breakfast for everyone with the fish that He'd just helped them catch.

Perhaps as they ate this breakfast around the little fire Jesus had built, Peter was recalling the time, not that long ago, when he denied the Lord by the glow of another fire.

Eventually, the Lord broke the silence. He asked Peter repeatedly, "Do you love Me?"

Peter had learned his lesson. Instead of boasting of his love for the Lord, he simply answered, "Yes Lord; You know that I love you" (John 21:15–17). The Greek word Peter used for "love" was *phileo,* a word for brotherly affection rather than the stronger love implied by the *agape* word that Jesus used in questioning Peter. Peter knew that his actions on the night Jesus was on trial had certainly not demonstrated true committed love for his Lord.

At least Peter was being honest.

How about you? We can talk all day about how much we love God, but fail when it comes to act upon it. Is your love for the Lord expressed more by your words than your actions?

My little children, let us not love in word
or in tongue, but in deed and in truth.

1 John 3:18

Peter eventually proved the true depth of his love for the Lord. He was a faithful apostle in the early church and wrote two New Testament letters. Historic tradition tells us that he died as a martyr for his faith, being crucified upside-down.

> The Lord's promise to His people...
>
> He who loves Me will be loved by My Father,
> and I will love him and manifest Myself to him.
> JESUS, IN JOHN 14:21

With God in prayer...

Give the Lord an honest assessment of your love for Him, as proven by your actions.

Because He loves you...

How is the Lord asking you to demonstrate your love for Him at this time?

Your own reflections... personal application... personal prayer points...

A CRITICAL BELIEF

I heard about a person in a spiritually weak church who sent this question to an advice columnist:

> Our preacher said on Easter that Jesus just swooned on the cross and that His disciples nursed Him back to health. What do you think?
> Sincerely,
> Bewildered

The columnist replied,

> Dear Bewildered:
> Beat your preacher with a cat of nine tails with 39 heavy strokes, nail him to a cross, hang him in the sun for six hours, run a spear through his side, embalm him, put him in an airless tomb for 36 hours, and see what happens.

What sets the Christian faith apart from all other beliefs and religious systems in this world?

When each of the founders of the world's religions died and was buried, their bodies stayed right where they were laid. But the tomb of Jesus Christ is empty, because He's alive.

We serve a *living* Savior!

Christ has been raised from the dead.
He has become the first of a great harvest
of those who will be raised to life again.
1 Corinthians 15:20 NLT

This is why the resurrection of Jesus is such an important message and also why it has been opposed so much throughout history. The devil knows that this resurrection spells his defeat. The devil also knows that if you believe this great truth that Jesus died on the cross for your sins and then rose from the dead, it can revolutionize your life.

> Just as Christ was raised from the dead by the glory of the Father, even so we also should walk in newness of life.
> Romans 6:4

Not only that, but putting your faith in Him also means that someday you'll have a new, resurrected body. As believers, we have this great hope that we, too, will overcome death.

> The Lord's promise to His people...
>
> He who raised Christ from the dead will also give life to your mortal bodies through His Spirit who dwells in you.
> ROMANS 8:11

With God in prayer...

How much "newness of life" (Romans 6:4) are you experiencing because of the resurrection of Christ? Talk with God about this.

Because He promises something new...

What's something "old" in your life that needs to be put aside and left behind as you live your life in Christ's resurrection power?

Your own reflections... personal application... personal prayer points...

NO REASON TO DOUBT

During the forty days from His resurrection to His ascension to heaven, Jesus was constantly appearing and vanishing before the disciples. I think He was getting the disciples accustomed to the fact that, even when He wasn't visible physically, He still would be present and available spiritually.

Before Jesus was crucified and resurrected, the disciples had expected the Messiah of Israel to come and establish an earthly kingdom, in which they would reign with Him. There was no doubt in their minds that Jesus was the Messiah, but when He was nailed to the cross, their conviction seemed like a colossal blunder.

Now, in the days following His resurrection, they began to realize how this was God's plan all along. Now they understood the prophecies of Scriptures—that the Messiah would first suffer before He was risen and glorified.

During this time, Jesus gave them this assignment: "Go and make disciples of all the nations, baptizing them in the name of the Father and the Son and the Holy Spirit. Teach these new disciples to obey all the commands I have given you" (Matthew 28:19–20 NLT).

After instructing His disciples to wait for the power they would receive from the Holy Spirit to be His worldwide witnesses, Jesus was taken up into heaven before their eyes (Acts 1:7–9). At that moment an angel appeared and told them, "Someday...he will return!" (Acts 1:11 NLT).

> While he was **blessing** them, he left them and was. taken up to heaven. They **worshiped** him and then returned to Jerusalem filled with great **joy**.
>
> Luke 24:51-52 NLT

BECAUSE....

The Father's promise, the Son's plans, and the Holy Spirit's power—all these would unite to turn these disciples into the most significant movement this world has ever seen.

Their lives would always be marked by *worship* of Jesus, *witnessing* for Jesus, and *waiting* for Jesus to return. Ours should be the same.

> The Lord's promise to His people...
>
> I go to prepare a place for you....
> I will come again and receive you to Myself.
> JESUS, IN JOHN 14:2–3

With God in prayer...

With joy, worship the Lord Jesus, who is risen and glorified.

Because Jesus is risen and glorified...

Take time today to evaluate your life in each of these three areas: *worship* of Jesus, *witnessing* for Jesus, and *waiting* for Jesus.

Your own reflections... personal application... personal prayer points...

NECESSARY ARMOR

When the apostle Paul wrote his letter to the Ephesians, he was chained to a Roman guard. So when we read this letter and come to his description of our spiritual armor (Ephesians 6:10–18), it's worth noting that he'd had a lot of time to observe Roman armor. There it was before his eyes, twenty-four hours a day—breastplate, helmet, shield, sword. Paul wasn't giving us some haphazard description off the top of his mind. There's significance behind every word.

Paul identifies six pieces of armor. The first three—belt, breastplate, and shoes—were for long-range protection and were never removed on the battlefield. The second three—shield, helmet, and sword—were kept in readiness for use when actual fighting began.

Use every piece of God's armor to resist the enemy in the time of evil, so that after the battle you will still be standing firm.

Ephesians 6:13 NLT

Let us who live in the light think clearly, protected by the body armor of faith and love, and wearing as our helmet the confidence of our salvation.

1 Thessalonians 5:8 NLT

Each piece was important. After all, you could be wearing helmet, breastplate, and shield, but without a sword, you were capable of only a defensive position. Or, you might have on your sandals and belt, with sword in hand for attacking enemy strongholds, yet quickly be overcome due to the lack of defensive protection provided by a shield and breastplate.

So we need *all* the armor. It's not for us to pick and choose; it's a package deal.

Think about this: Exactly why do you **need** spiritual armor?

God has given us clear and defined spiritual weapons to fight with. Understanding what they are and knowing how to use them can make all the difference in our spiritual battles.

The Lord's promise to His people...

The God of Israel is He who gives
strength and power to His people.
PSALM 68:35

With God in prayer...

Take time to read prayerfully through Ephesians 6:10–18. Ask the Lord to help you better understand what each piece of armor represents in your life.

Because He equips you for battle...

What's the most critical way in which you need to be spiritually strong at this time in your life? Where is the spiritual "battle" happening in your life right now? In this conflict, how can you more consciously rely on the Lord's armor?

Your own reflections... personal application... personal prayer points...

ARMED WITH TRUTH

In his description of the armor of God in Ephesians 6, Paul doesn't start with the high-profile objects like the sword or the shield. Instead, he begins his list by telling us to put on the "belt of truth."

> Stand your ground, putting on the sturdy belt of truth.
> Ephesians 6:14 NLT

What was Paul speaking of?

We need to think "Roman soldier" here for a moment. The Romans didn't wear pants like we do today. Their basic uniform was a loose, gown-like tunic. To move quickly in battle, the Roman soldier would gather and tuck the loose folds of his tunic beneath his tightened belt, which allowed for freer, faster movement.

The belt is not a dramatic piece of armor, but it was essential to everything else. The soldier's breastplate was attached to his belt, and so was the sheath for his sword. So if his belt loosened or slipped off, his breastplate and sword might fall off, and his clothing would come loose. You could be the best soldier on the field, but if you tripped over your own clothing and equipment, you would look rather foolish.

So the belt was important. That's why Paul put it at the top of the list.

This belt is the "belt of truth." How important is truth in your daily life? Are you facing and accepting the full truth about who you are and who the Lord is?

BECAUSE . . .

To have your belt tightened means you're ready for battle and ready to move. We need to be on duty at all times. We can't afford to take a few days off spiritually. We must keep our armor on at all times, because the moment we take it off is the moment the devil will be there to hit us with full force.

> The Lord's promise to His people...
>
> The truth is in Jesus.
>
> EPHESIANS 4:21

With God in prayer...

Ask God to show you any shortage of truth in the way you view yourself and those around you. His Holy Spirit is "the Spirit of truth" (John 14:17), and the Spirit will faithfully reveal this to you.

Because Jesus is the truth...

If the Holy Spirit shows you anything in your attitudes or perspectives that's based on anything less than the truth and reality, make the necessary changes *now* in your thinking.

Your own reflections... personal application... personal prayer points...

Wednesday

RIGHTEOUSNESS TO WEAR

Next in Paul's listing of the armor of God is the "breastplate of righteousness."

The breastplate protected the vital organs of a Roman soldier. It protected the part of his body that the enemy tried hardest to strike.

Stand therefore...having put on the breastplate of righteousness.
Ephesians 6:14

In the same way, Satan has his favorite targets when he attacks us spiritually.

We're often particularly vulnerable to such an attack after we've committed a sin, because the devil comes to us and says, "You've blown it! You aren't worthy of God's forgiveness! You don't deserve His blessings! God won't listen to your prayers, because you're a hypocrite."

What can you say when such an attack comes?

The truth is that we all fail at times. We all fall short. The Bible says, "If we say that we have no sin, we deceive ourselves, and the truth is not in us" (1 John 1:8).

So how can you answer the devil's accusations? Will you boast about how often you go to church or how many Bible verses you've memorized or how many people you've led to the Lord?

If you rely on such boasting, you're guilty of self-righteousness, which simply means you believe you somehow merit God's blessing because of all the good things you've done. If this is your attitude, you have a breastplate made of cardboard. One strike of the enemy's sword will cut it apart and leave you open and exposed.

50

When you've sinned and the enemy condemns and accuses you, don't try boasting of all you've done for God. Instead, *boast of all God has done for you.* That's what it means to put on the breastplate of righteousness.

The Lord's promise to His people...

Though your sins are like scarlet, they shall be as white as snow; though they are red like crimson, they shall be as wool.

ISAIAH 1:18

With God in prayer...

Give thanks to your Father in heaven that Jesus Christ Himself is *your* righteousness; He Himself "became for us wisdom from God—and righteousness and sanctification and redemption" (1 Corinthians 1:30).

Because Christ is your righteousness...

To keep yourself from getting spiritually paralyzed or discouraged after you've committed a sin, what do you need to do to arm yourself with "the breastplate of righteousness"? How can you hold on to the *fact* of your righteousness in Christ? Think through the best practical response.

Your own reflections... personal application... personal prayer points...

Thursday

THE RIGHT SHOES

No matter how powerful a Roman soldier's breastplate, or how much he'd tightened his belt, these wouldn't do much good if he stumbled and fell. Therefore, in Paul's list of the armor of God, he refers next to a soldier's footwear—and this represents being prepared with "the gospel of peace" (Ephesians 6:15).

Stand therefore...having shod your feet
with the preparation of the gospel of peace.
Ephesians 6:14–15

For shoes, put on the peace that comes
from the Good News, so that you will be fully prepared.
Ephesians 6:15 NLT

The Roman soldier's sandal or boot was essentially a leather sole with straps that wrapped tightly around the foot and ankle. The bottom was studded with nails, providing the soldier with better traction and thus preventing him from slipping and sliding on tricky terrain.

These battle sandals also provided mobility. These weren't dress shoes—only for show, and meant to be kept perfectly clean. No, these shoes were for action, allowing you to move anywhere at a moment's notice.

That's why Paul makes the connection to being ready with the gospel. As 1 Peter 3:15 tells us, "If you are asked about your Christian hope, always be ready to explain it" (NLT). Being prepared with the gospel of peace includes always being ready to give a defense of what we believe—always ready to seize opportunities to share the good news of Jesus Christ.

Some people say, "The Lord never opens up opportunities for me to share my faith." I think He does, but often we aren't paying attention. Opportunities are all around us, and we need to have our spiritual antenna up to recognize them when they come.

The armor of God is not only for holding your ground; it's also for gaining ground. We gain ground when we're prepared and can walk through the doors of opportunity God opens for us.

The Lord's promise to His people...

Peace I leave with you, My peace I give to you.
JESUS, IN JOHN 14:27

With God in prayer...

Ask God to open your eyes to the opportunities He provides to share the gospel with others—the gospel that brings such profound peace into hearts that are troubled, restless, and unsatisfied.

Because you are a messenger of the Lord's peace...

Who do you need to begin sharing the gospel with?

Your own reflections... personal application... personal prayer points...

Friday

THE SHIELD OF FAITH

What is the "shield of faith" Paul refers to in Ephesians 6?

In every battle you will need faith as your shield to stop
the fiery arrows aimed at you by Satan.

Ephesians 6:16 NLT

A Roman soldier's shield was made of wood, typically covered in leather. It was about four feet high and two feet wide.

This shield was particularly helpful when the enemy would fire a barrage of flaming arrows before the opposing armies were close enough for actual face-to-face engagement. Such an onslaught of blazing arrows could be very demoralizing and confusing.

The same goes for us. The devil will direct all kinds of flaming arrows toward Christians. They could be arrows of immorality, hatred, pride, envy, covetousness, doubt, worry, or any other kind of sin. They're delivered primarily in the realm of our thoughts. And they come at strategic times, like when we've decided to read the Bible or go to church, or when we need to be strong in order to endure times of trial and hardship.

It's during these attacks that you hold up the shield of faith—not the shield of *feelings,* not the shield of *emotions,* but the shield of *faith.*

Blessed are those who trust in the LORD
and have made the LORD their hope and confidence.

Jeremiah 17:7 NLT

BECAUSE . . .

You base your faith on what God has done for you, not on how you feel at a given moment. Emotions come and go—sometimes you feel great, sometimes you feel terrible, sometimes you don't feel anything.

In what ways do you rely **unwisely** on your feelings?

That's why you can't depend on feelings, but must instead learn to use faith—your full trust in the Lord and His promises—as your true protective shield.

> The Lord's promise to His people...
>
> Anyone who believes in him will not be disappointed.
> ROMANS 10:11 NLT

With God in prayer...

Confess to God how much you truly trust in Him. If you have any doubts, confess those as well.

Because He is worthy of your trust...

Identify the kinds of situations in which you're most likely to trust in your own unreliable feelings instead of in God and His truth. What can you do to change?

Your own reflections... personal application... personal prayer points...

WEAR YOUR HELMET

A lot of motorcyclists today don't like helmet laws. I'm among their ranks, I must say, because it's fun to get on a motorcycle and ride along with nothing on your head. But quite honestly, if you're in an accident on your bike and you become airborne, a helmet suddenly sounds like a really good idea. Helmets have saved the lives of many motorcyclists.

Helmets were also a life-and-death matter for Roman soldiers. The helmet protecting his head was made of leather shrouded in metal, and was designed to withstand a crushing blow to the head.

> And take the helmet of salvation.
>
> Ephesians 6:17

As believers, we need to put on the "helmet of salvation" because our minds, our thoughts, and our imaginations must be protected. It's here that most temptations start. Satan recognizes the value of first getting a foothold in the realm of the thoughts and imaginations, because this will prepare the way for those thoughts to translate into action. As the saying goes, "Sow a thought; reap an act. Sow an act; reap a habit. Sow a habit; reap a character. Sow a character; reap a destiny." It starts with a thought.

Are you protecting your thinking? Do you allow your thinking to be rooted and fully conditioned by the fact of your deliverance from sin that Jesus Christ accomplished on the cross?

While we cannot control all the things we're exposed to in this world, we can control a few things. We can control what we watch at home on television. We can control what movies we decide to see. We can control what we choose to read and what we listen to. Be careful, then, what you allow into your mind. Put on the helmet of salvation.

BECAUSE

> ·The Lord's promise to His people...
>
> God decided to save us through our Lord Jesus Christ,
> not to pour out his anger on us.
>
> 1 THESSALONIANS 5:9 NLT

With God in prayer...

Take time to thank God as fully as you can for the salvation He has won for you through the blood of His Son. Let this truth wash over your mind.

Because He saved you from sin...

Think ahead and review the choices you will likely need to make in the next twenty-four hours about the things that will significantly influence your thoughts. What decisions should you make to protect your mind with the helmet of salvation?

Your own reflections... personal application... personal prayer points...

Monday

REMEMBER YOUR SWORD

Many believers have all their defensive spiritual armor in place, but they never use their sword. They talk about this sword. They study it. They compare swords with others. But they never really *use* their sword in spiritual battle.

In fact, the devil would be pleased if believers would just keep their sword in its sheath. The devil knows too well the power and the authority of this sword—because it's God's Word, which is the sword of *the Spirit*.

> Take the **sword** of the Spirit, which is the **Word** of God.
> Ephesians 6:17 NLT

This sword is unequaled in its force and might: "For the word of God is full of living power. It is sharper than the sharpest knife, cutting deep into our innermost thoughts and desires. It exposes us for what we really are" (Hebrews 4:12 NLT). God wants us to fully appreciate this power of the Scriptures:

> "Is not My **word** like a fire?" says the LORD,
> "and like a hammer that **breaks** the rock in pieces?"
> Jeremiah 23:29

There's power and authority and effectiveness in the Word of God. That's why the devil doesn't want you to use this incredible weapon God has given you.

Remember how effectively Jesus used the sword of God's Word to defend Himself when He faced spiritual attack in the wilderness? Jesus

58

BECAUSE . . .

was God, so He didn't have to stand around and deal with the devil. He could have gotten out of the situation easily. Instead He stood and modeled for us the right way to fight temptation—with the Word of God.

So when the devil tries to attack you with temptations, fear, doubt, or memories of past sins which you've already confessed and of which you've been forgiven, remember the sword of the Spirit. Pull it out of its sheath and use it aggressively to defend yourself.

> The Lord's promise to His people...
>
> So shall My word be that goes forth from My mouth....
> It shall accomplish what I please, and it shall prosper
> in the thing for which I sent it.
>
> ISAIAH 55:11

With God in prayer...

Take time to read prayerfully through at least a portion of Psalm 119, and agree in prayer with the statements made there.

Because God's Word is your life...

How well are you doing in your intake of God's Word? Do you need to step it up? If so, how should you do that at this time?

Your own reflections... personal application... personal prayer points...

PLEASING GOD

Scripture tells us of a time in history when everyone's thoughts were "consistently and totally evil" (Genesis 6:5 NLT). People in those days were so wicked that God was sorry He ever created them.

Yet in the midst of this dark environment was an individual who shows us it's possible to live a godly life in an ungodly world. In this unique time in history, prior to God's judgment by the Flood, "Enoch walked with God" (Genesis 5:24). Enoch was so close to God that he was allowed to escape physical death—God lifted him from earth and took him directly into His presence.

> Enoch lived 365 years in all. He enjoyed a close
> relationship with God throughout his life.
> Then suddenly, he disappeared because God took him.
> Genesis 5:23-24 NLT

We see more about this same man in the New Testament, where we read the profound statement that Enoch "pleased God" (Hebrews 11:5).

We, too, can live our lives in a way that pleases God. How? Faithfully trusting in God—has to be a big part of it, because we read in the very next verse that "without faith it is impossible to please Him" (Hebrews 11:6).

Pleasing God involves prayer as well as action: "And whatever we ask we receive from Him, because we keep His commandments and do those things that are pleasing in His sight" (1 John 3:22).

Of course, as you read and study God's Word, you'll discover many other things that please Him.

Some people have the mistaken notion that God is difficult to please. He is not. He loves you and knows all about you. He is patient with you. Your failures don't come as a surprise to Him. He wants the best for you. And His resources are at your disposal to help you please Him more and more.

Enoch's life earned this commendation: "He pleased God." Can that also be said about you today?

The Lord's promise to His people...

The LORD your God...will rejoice over you with gladness.

ZEPHANIAH 3:17

With God in prayer...

Tell God all about your desire to please Him.

Because He's so worthy of being pleased...

Ask yourself this question: What about your life is *most* pleasing to God? What about your life is *least* pleasing to Him?

Your own reflections... personal application... personal prayer points...

Wednesday

FAITHFUL TO THE END

Today I want to look at one of the Bible's unsung heroes. His name was Caleb, and he never lost his edge, either spiritually or physically.

Caleb and Joshua were heroes when Moses included them in a group of spies sent into the Promised Land. (The story is told in Numbers 13). Decades later, when Caleb was eighty-five years old, he could say, "I am as strong now as I was when Moses sent me on that journey, and I can still travel and fight as well as I could then" (Joshua 14:11 NLT). Caleb had longevity.

He had spiritual longevity, too. The same passage tells us that Caleb "wholeheartedly followed the LORD, the God of Israel" (Joshua 14:14 NLT). To follow the Lord wholeheartedly means giving 100 percent to God. If we want spiritual longevity, we must do the same.

Envision yourself at age eighty-five. What do you want to be true about your spiritual life at that time?

Often when our lives are in trouble, we expect God to drop everything, run to us, and take care of our problems. But when it comes to us doing our part for Him, it's amazing how busy we can be. We think, "My schedule's so full. I don't have time for Bible study." We have tons of time for watching TV and reading magazines and talking on the phone, but not for the Word of God.

What percent of your time is truly available to God?

If your heart is right with God, it will show in the way you spend your time. It will show in the way you live your life.

If you're wholly following the Lord as Caleb did, you'll want to give God your best, not your leftovers. That was the secret to Caleb's spiritual longevity.

> The Lord's promise to His people...
>
> I will give them a heart to know Me, that I am the LORD;
> and they shall be My people, and I will be their God,
> for they shall return to Me with their whole heart.
>
> JEREMIAH 24:7

With God in prayer...

Worship God, giving all your heart to Him as best you know how.

Because God is worthy of your all...

Are you giving yourself 100 percent to the Lord? If not—where are you holding back? What should you do about this?

Your own reflections... personal application... personal prayer points...

Thursday

KEPT BY HIS LOVE

If you have young children, you wouldn't take them somewhere (like Disneyland) and turn them loose, forgetting where they are. You keep them with you or in your sight, because you protect those you love.

In the same way, God never forgets those He loves. As believers, we are those "who are called to live in the love of God the Father and the care of Jesus Christ" (Jude 1 NLT). That last phrase is also translated as "preserved in Jesus Christ" (NKJV) or "kept by Jesus Christ" (NIV).

Whatever the difficulties you face today, you need to know you're preserved in Christ, and He'll maintain His investment which He purchased at the cross. He'll protect you, preserve you, and keep you.

Yet God also tells us, in this same book of the Bible, to "keep yourselves in the love of God" (Jude 21). Is this a contradiction? No. It's merely two sides of the same coin. The Bible is teaching that God will keep us, but at the same time, we must keep ourselves in His love. We don't keep ourselves saved, but we keep ourselves safe.

There are things we must do on a daily basis to keep ourselves in a place where God can actively bless us, to keep ourselves away from all that's unlike Him, and from those things that would drag us down spiritually.

Are you in the right place to be actively **blessed** by God?

Attacks will come our way. Were it not for the preserving grace of God, none of us would make it. Clearly we're preserved, protected, and kept by the power of God. He "is able to keep you from stumbling" (Jude 24).

But God expects from us the right response to this grace and power that He bestows.

The Lord's promise to His people...

He shall give His angels charge over you,
to keep you in all your ways.

PSALM 91:11

With God in prayer...

Think about the ways you have greatly needed—and received—the Lord's protection recently. Thank Him fully for this care.

Because He cares for you...

In what areas of life do you need to step forward boldly and confidently, because of the certainty of the Lord's protection for you?

Your own reflections... personal application... personal prayer points...

AN ENDING I DIDN'T LIKE

Ever since childhood, I've always had a great admiration for the historical person known as Jesus. I'd seen movies about Him. I thought very highly of Him.

As a little boy, I lived with my grandmother for a few years. I would thumb through her big family Bible and look inside at the pictures of Jesus. She also had a picture of Jesus hanging on the wall. I would stare at it and think, "I wish I could have known that man Jesus."

But there was one thing I didn't like about His story. I didn't like how it ended. I thought it should have been rewritten with a happier ending. The part about Him being crucified wrecked everything. He was on this great roll, healing people and teaching people, but then it all came to an end. Why did they have to put Him on a cross and kill Him?

> Carrying the cross by himself, Jesus went to the place called Skull Hill (in Hebrew, Golgotha). There they crucified him.
>
> John 19:17-18 NLT

Only after I became a Christian did I realize that the crucifixion of Jesus actually was *the primary reason* Jesus came to this earth in the first place.

Jesus came to die. He spoke of His death frequently and in great detail. His arrest and crucifixion didn't take Him by surprise.

Jesus summed it up well when He told His disciples, "For even the Son of Man did not come to be served, but to serve, and *to give His life* a ransom for many" (Mark 10:45).

How regularly do you give **thanks** to the Lord for **saving you** from condemnation in hell?

BECAUSE...

67

Jesus was born to die that we might live. The gift of eternal life is offered freely to us because Jesus purchased it with His death.

Have you fully embraced that gift? Thank Him again for it this very moment.

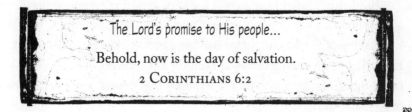

The Lord's promise to His people...

Behold, now is the day of salvation.

2 CORINTHIANS 6:2

With God in prayer...

Knowing how committed Jesus was to obeying His Father even to the point of death on the cross...give Him praise for that commitment.

Because Jesus gave His all...

Remember again: Jesus came "to serve, and to give His life a ransom." The ransom is paid, once for all. And now Jesus calls us to follow His example in serving others, as He did. Who does God want you to serve *today*, in Jesus' name? How can you serve them?

Your own reflections... personal application... personal prayer points...

Weekend

ONLY ACTING?

Of the twelve disciples, we envision Judas Iscariot as the one with shifty eyes, lurking in the shadows. With the other disciples wearing white, we see Judas in black. We're sure we would have immediately recognized him as the bad guy.

But I think Judas Iscariot was the very opposite—a phenomenal actor who came across as an upright man, devout in his faith.

As one of the Twelve, Judas had been handpicked by the Lord Himself, but eventually betrayed Him for a few pieces of silver. Judas made the wrong choice to do the wrong thing, though he'd been exposed to so much truth.

> Then Satan entered into Judas Iscariot....
> He began looking for an opportunity to betray Jesus.
> Luke 22:3, 6 NLT

With his own ears Judas heard Jesus deliver the Sermon on the Mount. With his own eyes he saw Jesus walk on water. He saw Lazarus raised from the dead. He saw the multitudes fed with a few loaves and fishes. He saw the blind receive their sight.

Judas saw it all. He heard it all. Yet he became more hardened in his unbelief.

Judas descended deeper into sin because *he really never knew Jesus.*

If you're a true Christian and you begin to compromise, you'll sense the conviction of the Holy Spirit. But if you can sin without any remorse, then one must question if you really know God. The true child of God, though still a sinner, simply will not live in a pattern of sin.

Those who have been born into God's family do not sin, because God's life is in them. So they can't keep on sinning, because they have been born of God.

1 John 3:9 NLT

If you find yourself, as a follower of Christ, immediately experiencing conviction when you start to sin, then rejoice. It's a reminder that you belong to the Lord.

The Lord's promise to His people...

Sin shall not have dominion over you.

ROMANS 6:14

With God in prayer...

What conviction of sin is the Spirit bringing to your attention?

Because He's faithful to convict you of sin...

What must you do today to turn from the sin the Lord is convicting you of?

Your own reflections... personal application... personal prayer points...

A CROSS WITHOUT JESUS?

A true story was reported about a woman visiting a jewelry store. As the jeweler showed her various crosses, she said to him, "I like these, but do you have any without this little man on them?"

That's what so many people want today—a cross without Jesus. They want a cross without any offense, one that looks cool with their outfits.

> The message of the cross is **foolishness** to those who are perishing, but to us who are being saved it is the **power** of God.
>
> 1 Corinthians 1:18

But if we could travel back in time and see the cross in its original context, we would realize how bloody and vile it was. To see someone hanging on a cross would have been the worst scene imaginable.

The Romans chose crucifixion as a form of execution because it was a slow, torturous way to die. It was designed to humiliate the victim. These shameful crucifixions were carried out on the roadways just outside cities throughout the empire, serving as warnings to anyone who would dare oppose Rome's rule.

> Take time to think deeply about the shame that Jesus **endured** throughout the day when He went to the **cross.**

If there was any other way to accomplish our salvation, do you think God would have allowed His Son to suffer like this? If there had been any other way to accomplish forgiveness for us, then God surely would have found it. If our living a good moral life would get us to heaven, then

Jesus would never have gone to the cross and died for us. But He did go, and He did die, because there was and is no other way. He had to pay the price for our sin. At the cross, Jesus purchased the salvation of the world.

If you were ever tempted to doubt God's love for you, even for a moment, then take a long, hard look at the cross. Nails didn't hold Jesus to that cross. His love did.

> The Lord's promise to His people...
>
> Nothing can ever separate us from his love.
> ROMANS 8:38 NLT

With God in prayer...

Confess to the Lord whatever ways you might have failed to fully appreciate His love for you.

Because of everything Jesus endured...

Just as Jesus endured the shame of the cross...what is He calling *you* to endure at this time?

Your own reflections... personal application... personal prayer points...

Tuesday

ULTIMATE SACRIFICE

I heard a story about a man who operated a railroad drawbridge over a large river. At a certain time every afternoon, he raised the bridge for a ferryboat to pass through, then lowered it in time for a passenger train to cross over. He performed this task precisely, according to the clock.

One day he brought his son along to watch him as he worked. As his father became occupied raising the bridge, the boy got excited and wanted to take a closer look. When his father realized his son was missing and began looking for him, he discovered to his horror that his son had wandered dangerously close to the bridge's gears, where he would be crushed if the bridge was let down. Frantic, he wanted to rush out and rescue the boy. But the passenger train was now approaching, and the bridge needed to be lowered at once.

The man faced a dilemma. If he lowered the bridge, his son would be killed. If he left it raised, hundreds of others would die. He knew what he had to do. And he did it.

A moment later, with tears streaming down his face, he watched the passenger train roll by. Through its windows he saw two women chatting over tea. Other passengers were reading newspapers. All were unaware of what had just transpired. None of them heard as the man cried out, "Do you realize I just gave my son for you?"

This story is a similar picture of what happened at the cross. God gave up His beloved Son so we might live. But most people seldom give it a thought.

Christ Jesus came into the world to **save** sinners.

1 Timothy 1:15

For there is one God and one Mediator
between God and men, the Man Christ Jesus.

1 Timothy 2:5

How about you? Are you conscious throughout each day of the
ultimate sacrifice God made on your behalf? Do you make sure to thank
Him?

> The Lord's promise to His people...
>
> For the wages of sin is death, but the gift
> of God is eternal life in Christ Jesus our Lord.
>
> ROMANS 6:23

With God in prayer...

Though the train passengers in that drawbridge story did not realize
their lives had just been saved, you and I *do* know what was done to save
us from something far worse than physical death. Speak with God your
Father to praise Him for His heart of love in saving you from sin's eternal
penalty.

Because God so loved the world...

In your world, who needs to know about the sacrifice God accomplished
to save human beings from hell? When can you tell them about this?

Your own reflections... personal application... personal prayer points...

HOW TO LOVE GOD

When Jesus says we're to love the Lord our God with all our *heart* (in Mark 12:30), He uses the word *heart* in reference to the core of our personal being. To love the Lord with all our hearts means to love Him with everything we are in the deepest parts of our being.

He tells us also to love the Lord our God with all our *soul*. That word speaks of emotion. It's the same word Jesus used when He cried out in the garden of Gethsemane, saying, "My soul is exceedingly sorrowful, even to death." Therefore we know that loving God includes our emotions.

Jesus also says we're to love God with all our *mind*. This word speaks of mental energy and strength, as well as intellectual commitment and determination. We love Him with our intellect. We love Him with our ability to reason.

Finally Jesus commands us to love God with all our *strength*—our physical energy and vitality and endurance.

> "You shall love the Lord your God with all your heart, with all your soul, with all your mind, and with all your strength."
> This is the first commandment.
>
> Jesus, in Mark 12:30

So you see, loving the Lord includes every part of our lives.

Now it seems as though some people are a bit off-balance in all this. They may love the Lord with all their minds, but they're afraid to express emotion to Him. Others love God but always seem to operate on raw emotion.

We need to find the balance. God wants us to love Him with every fiber of our being.

> The Lord's promise to His people...
>
> All things work together for good to those who love God.
> ROMANS 8:28

With God in prayer...

Read prayerfully through the first two verses of Psalm 18. Use these words of David as your own expression of love to the Lord.

Because love involves every part of who we are...

Are you in proper balance in the way you love God? Evaluate especially how well you are loving Him emotionally, intellectually, and physically.

Your own reflections... personal application... personal prayer points...

Thursday

AS YOU LOVE YOURSELF

When Jesus said, "Love your neighbor as yourself," He wasn't saying you must first love yourself before you can love others. That's a common interpretation we often hear of this passage, but it isn't correct. Jesus is not teaching self-love. Essentially, He's saying that just as you *already* love yourself, as you *already* care for yourself and think about yourself, you're to love your neighbor in the same way.

> You shall love your neighbor as yourself.
>
> Jesus, in Mark 12:31

We already love ourselves. As the apostle Paul said, "No one hates his own body but lovingly cares for it" (Ephesians 5:29 NLT). How true that is!

Sometimes people say, "I hate myself. I'm so ugly (or weak or unhappy or stupid, or whatever it is). I'm just so horrible that I just hate myself." Really? If you truly hated yourself, you would be happy you were ugly or stupid, right?

Why is it that people who say they hate themselves spend all their time talking about themselves? "I hate the way I look," they'll say. "I hate the way I feel about myself. I hate that I can't do this or that."

No, the fact of the matter is that all the attention they shower on their own lives *proves* they love themselves. The truth is, we *all* love ourselves.

What convinces you that you do, indeed, love **yourself**?

Jesus is saying, "You already love yourself; therefore, love your neighbor." He goes on to say that if you do this, as well as love the Lord with all your heart, all your soul, all your mind, and all your strength, then all the commandments of God will be fulfilled, because you'll naturally do the things that please Him.

The Lord's promise to His people...

Your love for one another will prove to the world that you are my disciples.

JESUS, IN JOHN 13:35 NLT

With God in prayer...

Loving others requires practical action, including prayer. In nearness to God, pray for the people God wants you to pray for.

Because love is the proof...

What does God want you to do *today* to demonstrate love to others?

Your own reflections... personal application... personal prayer points...

SATAN'S OPEN DOORS

When Judas Iscariot turned his back on Jesus, he had little trouble getting help for his plan. The Bible says the authorities were "glad" when Judas approached them, and they quickly dangled a financial reward before his eyes.

Judas must have thought, *This is going easier than I thought was possible!* As he stood before those smiling religious leaders, perhaps Judas even told himself, *This must be God's will!*

> Then Judas Iscariot, one of the twelve, went to the chief priests to **betray** Him to them. And when they heard it, they were glad, and promised to give him money. So he sought how he might conveniently betray **Him**.
> Mark 14:10-11

We must realize something here: Satan opened all the doors for Judas's betrayal of Jesus. It's amazing how skilled Satan is at manipulating circumstances to facilitate our disobedience. God isn't the only one who can open doors. But circumstances manipulated by the devil will always lead us to entrapment and disaster.

I've had people walk up to me and say, "The Lord brought this wonderful person into my life." I'll ask whether this person is a Christian. "No, but I know the *Lord* gave me this person—I was praying, and it happened. It *must* be God's will." It hasn't occurred to them that the devil might have brought someone along to influence them the wrong way.

Are you quick to let circumstances guide and influence your decisions and plans, without weighing everything against God's Word? If so, you're being foolish, because "circumstances" can easily be part of the devil's deceptive tactics.

"Your adversary the devil walks about like a roaring lion" (1 Peter 5:8)—and while he's at it, be sure that he'll make it as easy as possible for you to make unwise decisions that will harm you.

> The Lord's promise to His people...
>
> Resist the devil and he will flee from you.
>
> JAMES 4:7

With God in prayer...

Ask God to help you clearly view your current circumstances in life from *His* perspective.

Because you can't trust circumstances to guide you...

What commands in God's Word relate most clearly to the biggest decisions you now are facing?

Your own reflections... personal application... personal prayer points...

FOR SUCH A TIME AS THIS

The book of Esther contains a wonderful and dramatic story of a beautiful young Jewish woman named Esther. She actually won a beauty contest, and as a result, was made queen of the kingdom. She was taken into the palace of the king, where she could enjoy the finest food, wear the most beautiful clothing, and have numerous servants to do her bidding. She was living in the lap of luxury.

But there was a wicked man named Haman working for the king. He hated the Jewish people and devised a wicked plot to exterminate all the Jews living in the kingdom. Haman was going about his business, seeing to it that his plan would come to pass.

Esther had an uncle named Mordecai, who was concerned that although his niece was in a place where she could influence the king to turn away from Haman's horrible plan, she was afraid to act. So Mordecai sent this message to Esther:

Do not think in your heart that you will escape in the king's palace any more than all the other Jews. For if you remain completely silent at this time, relief and deliverance will arise for the Jews from another place, but you and your father's house will perish. *Yet who knows whether you have come to the kingdom for such a time as this?* (Esther 4:13–14).

Stirred by this message, Esther went to the king and appealed to him, and Haman's wicked plot was averted.

As for me, I trust in You, O Lord....
My times are in Your hand.
Psalm 31:14-15

If you're in a difficult place, who knows whether God hasn't put you there right now *for such a time as this?*

So in whatever situation you find yourself, seize the moment. Do what you can—just as Esther boldly did.

The Lord's promise to His people...

To everything there is a season, a time for every purpose under heaven....
A time to plant...a time to heal...a time to build up...
a time to embrace...a time to gain...a time to speak...
a time to love...a time of war, and a time of peace.
ECCLESIASTES 3:1–8

With God in prayer...

Enter God's presence to prayerfully learn more of exactly *why* you are in your current circumstances and location.

Because His placement and timing are perfect...

What is now the most significant opportunity you need to seize in obeying God's will and serving His kingdom?

Your own reflections... personal application... personal prayer points...

Monday

THE GOODNESS OF GOD

One thing that's clear in the Bible is that God is good. We see this truth demonstrated again and again. And God wants us to truly experience His goodness, just as David says: "Oh, taste and see that the LORD is good" (Psalm 34:8).

> Oh, give thanks to the Lord, for He is good!
> For His mercy endures forever.
> Psalm 118:1

God's goodness fully includes His plans for our future. "For I know the thoughts that I think toward you, says the LORD, thoughts of peace and not of evil, to give you a future and a hope" (Jeremiah 29:11).

Of course, God has an obvious advantage over all of us. He has complete foreknowledge. He knows everything that will happen in our lives; therefore He's trying to mold us into men and women of God, as He unfolds His plan for our lives as individuals.

Maybe we *don't* think God is good. Maybe we think God is out to ruin our lives. If you sometimes come to that conclusion, perhaps it's because someone has misrepresented God to you somewhere along the line. Maybe it was a bad experience in church, or it was a pastor or Sunday school teacher who did or said something that disillusioned you.

Then again, maybe you had a father who mistreated you and abused you. Sadly, this happens a lot in our culture. Many children today come from broken homes in which their fathers have neglected them or even abandoned them. Perhaps you've seen those traits of your earthly father and projected them onto your heavenly Father.

But you need to know something: God *is* good. Realize this truth about His nature, and realize and embrace this truth about His purposes for your life.

> The Lord's promise to His people...
>
> My people shall be satisfied with
> My goodness, says the LORD.
> JEREMIAH 31:14

With God in prayer...

"Give thanks to the LORD, for He is good!" (Psalm 106:1, 107:1). If you have any doubts about God's goodness, confess those to Him.

Because God is good...

What can you do today to demonstrate your trust in the goodness of the future God has planned for you?

Your own reflections... personal application... personal prayer points...

CRY OUT FOR HIS HELP

The Bible tells the story of Simon Peter walking on the water with Jesus (Matthew 14:28–33). He was doing it! But once he began to realize the impossibility of the situation, he started sinking.

And he cried out, "Lord, save me!"

How easily Jesus could have answered, "You got yourself in this situation; now get yourself out of it. Swim!" But instead the Bible says, "Immediately Jesus stretched out His hand and caught him" (Matthew 14:31). *Immediately.* I like that.

When you begin to sink, and the cry "Lord, save me!" comes right from your heart, He'll immediately reach out to you. But you must cry out for His help, and that's hard for some of us to do.

> I love the **Lord** because he hears and **answers** my prayers.
>
> Psalm 116:1 NLT

As a kid, I spent a lot of time at the beach. When I was out bodysurfing one day, a big set of waves started coming in. So I did what I was supposed to do: I swam toward the waves and went under them. When I looked up, there was another set. I swam under those too. One set after another came.

Finally I was so far out that people I saw on the beach looked like little ants. But I was exhausted. I had no strength left. I had nothing to hold onto.

I was in trouble.

I realized I had two choices. One, I could cry out and wave for help, and the lifeguard would come out with his life preserver; when he got me to shore, my friends would laugh at me, and I would never live it down. Or two, I could drown with dignity.

The **Lord** is near to all who call upon Him,
to all who call upon Him in **truth**.

Psalm 145:18

A lot of us don't want to admit our need. We don't want to cry out to God. We want to maintain our dignity, even if it means drowning.

But I need the best God has to offer. And you do too.

> The Lord's promise to His people...
>
> Call upon Me in the day of trouble;
> I will deliver you, and you shall glorify Me.
> PSALM 50:15

With God in prayer...

Find a secluded place where you can privately pray and speak *aloud* to the Lord, telling Him of your true needs at this time.

Because He hears your cry for help...

Is there anything that you're pridefully holding on to, anything that's preventing you from admitting a true need to the Lord? If you recognize that there is such a block in your life, let go of it today.

Your own reflections... personal application... personal prayer points...

Wednesday

HUMBLE HEARING

The Word of God cannot work in our lives unless we receive it in the right way. It's possible to hear God's Word with our ears, but not with our hearts.

James tells us to "receive with meekness the implanted word, which is able to save your souls" (James 1:21). The picture is one of soil. The human heart is like receptive soil for the implanted seed of the Word of God.

We determine what kind of soil our hearts will have by our response to God's Word. That's why James says in the same verse, "Lay aside all filthiness and overflow of wickedness." For the seed of God's Word to take root properly, we must first clear the ground of all that would hinder its growth. We need to uproot weeds of bitterness, wickedness, or anything that would keep the seed from taking root.

> Break up your fallow ground, and do not SOW among thorns.
>
> Jeremiah 4:3

Once the ground is broken up and cleared out, what are we to do? "Receive with meekness the implanted word." This would be the opposite of pride. It means coming humbly, with an open ear, to apply God's precious Word, and not with some hypercritical, already-heard-that attitude. It's an openness to the Word of God.

> Why do you think humility is so necessary in truly being able to hear God speak?

After years of walking with the Lord, the apostle Paul made this humble statement: "Not that I have already attained, or am already perfected; but I press on, that I may lay hold of that for which Christ Jesus has also laid hold of me" (Philippians 3:12).

There's so much to learn, so much to know. We need to come to God's Word with a willingness to accept and apply what it says.

The Lord's promise to His people...

He leads the humble in what is right, teaching them his way.
PSALM 25:9 NLT

With God in prayer...

We're commanded in James 4:10, "Humble yourselves in the sight of the Lord." Seek to learn more about how to do this as you get alone with God.

Because God speaks to those who humbly hear...

What has God already spoken clearly to you about that you now need to act upon?

Your own reflections... personal application... personal prayer points...

GETTING SERIOUS AGAINST SIN

I read a newspaper article about a hungry thief who grabbed some sausages in a meat market. What he didn't realize was that the sausages were part of a several-foot long string. As he was making his getaway, he tripped over them and couldn't escape. The police found him collapsed in a tangle of sausages. He was literally caught in the act.

In the same way, many people today play with sin, thinking they'll get away with it. If they don't get caught at first, they'll go and do it over and over again.

Sometimes people misinterpret God's loving patience and willingness to forgive as leniency. They think God is a soft touch, a pushover. Because they get away with their sin, they think God doesn't really mind. Then they deceive themselves into thinking God approves of what they're doing.

> Should we keep on **sinning** so that God can show us more
> and more kindness and **forgiveness**? Of course not!
> Since we have died to sin, how can we continue to live in it?
>
> Romans 6:1-2 NLT

We must not misinterpret God's mercy as God's lenience. The Bible says, "The Lord is not slack concerning His promise, as some count slackness, but is longsuffering toward us, not willing that any should perish but that all should come to repentance" (2 Peter 3:9).

Is God cutting you slack right now? If you're committing a sin that hasn't yet caught up with you, please don't misperceive that as leniency. Recognize it as *mercy*. Recognize that, sooner or later, it will catch up with you.

The best thing you can do is turn from that sin, run to Jesus, fall down at His feet, and ask for His mercy. But if you continue, you'll one day discover that your sin will find you out.

> The Lord's promise to His people...
>
> Trouble chases sinners, while blessings chase the righteous!
> PROVERBS 13:21 NLT

With God in prayer...

Talk with God about any sin that you've been "playing with" without "getting caught." Confess it for the ugly reality that it is in God's sight.

Because sin cannot be hidden...

Repent—turn away—from any sin that you've been "playing with." Decide what must be done to put this sin out of your sight, and out of God's.

Your own reflections... personal application... personal prayer points...

THE ESSENTIAL QUESTION

Imagine boarding an airplane, finding your seat, then hearing the pilot greet you with these words:

"Ladies and gentlemen, welcome to Flight 239 with service to Honolulu, Hawaii. Our cruising altitude today will be 22,000 feet.

"By the way, folks, on our trip over the ocean I don't plan to use any of this plane's navigation devices, because, you know, that would be so narrow, so absolute. I believe we can just go with the flow—because, you know, all air streams lead to Hawaii.

"And another thing—as I look at the fuel gauge, it doesn't appear we have enough to get to Hawaii. But I want you to know I have a good feeling about this, so there's no need to panic.

"And please don't get upset with me or criticize me about any of this, because believe me, I'm very sincere in what I'm saying.

"Have a good flight!"

Of course you would rise from your seat and say, "I'm getting off this plane—right now!"

Yet when it comes to the things of God, to matters with eternal ramifications, people make statements like that pilot's words. People want to believe all roads lead to God, and that if they're sincere enough, whatever path they choose will eventually get them there. But religious belief systems are all different; they largely contradict each other, and all the others conflict with Christianity on the most essential point—their view of Jesus Christ and His authority. Therefore, they can't all be true.

My Father has given me authority over everything.

Jesus, in Matthew 11:27 NLT

You can't say all roads are the same, or that all religions teach the same thing, because they don't. Only one can be true.

So you must make the decision about who you'll believe, because that's what it comes down to.

Hundreds of years ago, Jesus asked His disciples a question: "Who do you say I am?" (Matthew 16:15 NLT). He's still asking that question today.

The Lord's promise to His people...

At the name of Jesus every knee will bow...and every tongue will confess that Jesus Christ is Lord, to the glory of God the Father

PHILIPPIANS 2:10–11 NLT

With God in prayer...

In reality, who do *you* say Jesus Christ is? Talk to Him about this.

Because Jesus Christ is the only Lord and Savior...

Who can you talk with today about Jesus—someone who needs to know that He is our only way to salvation?

Your own reflections... personal application... personal prayer points...

THE CHOICE WE MUST MAKE

Christianity is not the most popular way to live. If you truly follow Jesus Christ, you'll be a part of a minority. After all, Jesus did say, "Narrow is the gate and difficult is the way which leads to life, and there are few who find it" (Matthew 7:14).

And in case you haven't noticed, it's open season on followers of Jesus. Christians are ridiculed and discriminated against. Christianity is misrepresented. The message of the gospel is distorted, suppressed, ignored.

So if you truly and wholeheartedly follow Jesus Christ, you'll have certain difficulties in life that you otherwise would avoid. And yet, although it's true that it costs to follow Jesus, it's also true that it costs a whole lot more *not* to follow Him. Whatever it costs to follow Jesus Christ, it's worth it. And whatever you give up, He'll make up to you.

> He who is not **with** Me is against Me,
> and he who does not **gather** with Me scatters.
>
> Jesus, in Luke 11:23

But you have to choose. When we come to the message of the gospel, we must say either yes or no to it. No maybes, no whatevers. Either we're in or we're out. Either we're for Jesus Christ, or we're against Him.

Have you given the Lord your **unqualified** yes?

Moses told the people of Israel, "I call heaven and earth as witnesses today against you, that I have set before you life and death, blessing and cursing; therefore choose life" (Deuteronomy 30:19).

After Joshua led God's people into the Promised Land, he confronted them: "Choose for yourselves this day whom you will serve.... But as for me and my house, we will serve the LORD" (Joshua 24:15).

On Mount Carmel, Elijah challenged the people with the same choice: "How long will you falter between two opinions? If the LORD is God, follow Him; but if Baal, follow him" (1 Kings 18:21).

We, too, must make a choice.

The Lord's promise to His people...

The LORD searches all hearts and understands all the intent of the thoughts. If you seek Him, He will be found by you; but if you forsake Him, He will cast you off forever.

1 CHRONICLES 28:9

With God in prayer...

Renew your commitment of your life to the Lord. Give Him your fullest "Yes."

Because you must choose...

Are there any pursuits, comforts, selfish pleasures, or unproductive relationships God is calling you to leave behind? If so, take that step today.

Your own reflections... personal application... personal prayer points...

Monday

MORE LISTENING, LESS TALKING

How different our lives would be if we heeded the admonition of James 1:19—"Be swift to hear, slow to speak, slow to wrath." Most of us do just the opposite: We're swift to speak, slow to listen, and quick to anger.

In this day of instant information when we don't need to wait for much of anything, it's hard to slow down and listen—especially to God. Many of us are like Martha as we see her in Luke 10; we run around in our little self-made circles of activity instead of calmly sitting at the Lord's feet like her sister Mary. We need to be quick to listen.

How **accurately** does "swift to hear, slow to speak" describe you?

We also need to be slow to speak. How many times have you blurted out something, only to regret it the moment it left your lips? Right after you said it, did you wonder why? Sometimes you want to say the right thing, but what comes out could hardly be worse. It's easier to save face if you simply keep your mouth shut more often. As the saying goes, "A closed mouth gathers no foot."

In the multitude of words sin is not **lacking**,
but he who **restrains** his lips is **wise**.
Proverbs 10:19

It has been estimated that most people speak enough words in one week to fill a five hundred-page book. In an average lifetime, this amounts to three thousand volumes, or 1.5 million pages. Can you imagine a record like that? It would appear that there is one—in heaven.

BECAUSE

Consider this warning from Jesus: "For every idle word men may speak, they will give account of it in the day of judgment" (Matthew 12:36).

There's no better reason to be quick to listen, slow to speak, and slow to anger.

> The Lord's promise to His people...
>
> He who guards his mouth preserves his life,
> but he who opens wide his lips shall have destruction.
> PROVERBS 13:3

With God in prayer...

Are you "swift to hear, slow to speak" when it comes to your communication with God? If not, take time today to allow God to restore the proper balance.

Because listening is more valuable than talking...

In what relationships or situations are you most likely to neglect careful listening to the other person? How can you change this situation?

Your own reflections... personal application... personal prayer points...

FAITH THAT WORKS

It may come as a surprise to you that the devil and his demons are neither atheists nor agnostics. They believe in the existence of God. They believe in the deity of Jesus Christ. They believe the Bible is the very Word of God. They believe Jesus is coming back again. You could say, in a limited sense, that the devil and his demons are quite orthodox in their beliefs.

But are they followers of Christ? No. They are opposed to the Lord.

Of course, we know that the devil is God's enemy. And we already know about the devil's fall, his evil agenda, and the certainty of his final, impending judgment. Yet the Bible says that he and his demons "believe"—in the sense that they would recognize certain truths as being accurate.

> Do you still think it's **enough** just to believe that there is one God? Well, even the demons believe this, and they tremble in **terror!**
>
> James 2:19 NLT

So you see, just because you believe something to be true doesn't necessarily mean you have real faith. You can even have a belief that's relatively orthodox, but in and of itself this is not enough. Such a belief is important, but not sufficient. *True faith must impact your life.*

It comes down to not just acknowledging something to be true, but actually following the Lord and being obedient to His Word.

Faith and "works" (our obedient actions and deeds) go together like two wings of an airplane. A person on a plane could say, "I really like the right wing better." Another person could say, "Well, I prefer the left wing." Personally I like both wings, because if one's missing, we aren't going anywhere. Both have their purpose—just like faith and works.

What is important is faith expressing itself in love.

Galatians 5:6 NLT

You can't have real faith without *doing* something; faith that's real will always impact the way you live.

> The Lord's promise to His people...
>
> I know your works, love, service, faith, and your patience.
> JESUS, IN REVELATION 2:19

With God in prayer...

Express your gratitude to the Lord for how your faith in Him truly has impacted your life.

Because faith without works is dead...

How does your faith need to go to work *today?*

Your own reflections... personal application... personal prayer points...

Wednesday

BALANCE IN SPIRITUAL GIFTS

Through the years, I've made my periodic trips to the gym to get back in shape. On one such occasion after I joined a local gym, a trainer took me on a tour to show me the various machines and how they worked. (Some of them are a little difficult to figure out these days!)

One thing the trainer mentioned especially caught my attention. He explained that it's important to work out every part of your body so you have a balanced physique. To fail to do so, he said, causes imbalance. A person needs cardiovascular exercises as well as strength training.

As the trainer began to describe the importance of balance and how the entire body needed exercise and training for good overall performance, I began to think about the body of Christ. We, too, need overall balance. And in our own personal lives as Christians, the key is balance.

> Now concerning **spiritual** gifts...I do not want you to be **ignorant**.
> 1 Corinthians 12:1

In Romans 12, we find that God has distributed gifts of the Holy Spirit into the lives of believers for the benefit of the whole church. Because of the abuse of these gifts by some, many believers have recoiled from these wonderful gifts God has given. As they see the excesses of those who have unwisely overemphasized these gifts, they think, *I don't want anything to do with that.*

> Now there are **different** kinds of spiritual gifts,
> but it is the same Holy Spirit who is the **source** of them all.
> 1 Corinthians 12:4 NLT

BECAUSE . . .

However, you can go too far in that direction also. The gifts of the Spirit are real, and they're available for Christians today. We should be seeking the gift or gifts He has placed in our lives, and we should be using them. "Pursue love, and desire spiritual gifts" (1 Corinthians 14:1).

The Lord's promise to His people...

A spiritual gift is given to each of us as a means of helping the entire church.

1 CORINTHIANS 12:7, NLT

With God in prayer...

Give thanks to the Lord for the Holy Spirit, and for the spiritual gifts He gives to all who are in His church, including you.

Because He's the Giver of gifts...

How well are you putting to good use the gifting you have received from God through His Holy Spirit? Wisely and in balance? Or have you neglected His gift?

Your own reflections... personal application... personal prayer points...

Thursday

THE "BEST" GIFTS

What are the best spiritual gifts for a believer to have? It all depends.

If I'm having a difficult time sharing my faith with someone, and you come along and have been gifted as an evangelist, that's the best gift at that particular moment.

But then let's say I'm trying to understand the meaning of a particular passage of Scripture, and God has given you the gift of teaching. For you to come and help me could be a great benefit.

Then again, let's say I'm undertaking a complex project, and I need help. What I really need is someone with the gift of helping or administration—and if that's you, you're the man of the hour.

> Having then gifts differing according to the grace that is given to us, let us use them.
> Romans 12:6

Or, let's say I'm lying in a hospital bed, and I'm discouraged. I don't really need a Bible study. I don't need someone to come and help me organize my life. I need someone with the gift of exhortation or encouragement. I need someone to come and help me sense that God still cares for me, and is still in control of my life.

Each one of these gifts is important, as God has distributed them.

We make a big mistake when we think some gifts are not really significant. They all have their place, and God has given them as He has chosen. Therefore, we need to pray, "Lord, what are my gifts? Help me to discover them. Help me to develop them. Help me to use them."

One day when you stand before God, you'll be held accountable for what He called you to do and for the resources He has provided you. And one day, He'll reward you for how faithful you were with what He gave you.

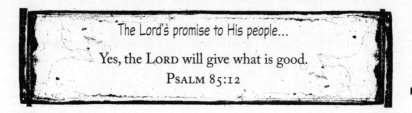

The Lord's promise to His people...

Yes, the LORD will give what is good.

PSALM 85:12

With God in prayer...

Ask God to help you fully understand the ways in which He has spiritually gifted you.

Because He's the Giver of gifts...

Carefully evaluate your faithfulness in how you've used the gifts and resources the Lord has given you.

Your own reflections... personal application... personal prayer points...

TO FILL YOUR MIND AND HEART

My computer screen flashes a little warning sign on those occasions when I try to load too much information on my hard drive. It tells me my memory is full—there's no more room for any more information.

In the same way, if we would fill our hearts and minds with God's Word, then when the devil comes with his perverse thoughts and ungodly schemes, he'll see a sign notifying him that our memory is full. That's why it's so important for us to fill our minds and hearts with the Word of God!

Certainly it's good to carry a Bible in your briefcase, pocket, or purse; but the best place to carry the Word of God is in your heart.

It's good to go through the Word of God; but the Word of God must go through you.

It's great to mark your Bible; but your Bible must mark you. It must affect the way you live.

Your **word** I have hidden in my heart, that I might not sin against You.... I will not forget Your word.... I trust in Your word.... Your word has given me life.... I **rejoice** at Your word as one who finds great **treasure**.

Psalm 119:11,16,42,50,162

One of the best ways I've found to remember Scripture is to write it down. I remember it more easily that way. In fact, the Bible tells us to store up these words in our hearts, teach them to our children, and write them down (see Deuteronomy 11:18–20).

Maybe when you're memorizing a verse, it doesn't feel like the most supernatural experience of your life. But it's a discipline. And the next time you're faced with a difficult situation, suddenly that verse will come to you with freshness from the throne of God. It will speak to your situation and strengthen your heart.

So get God's Word into your heart and mind. And that will make it easier to put it into practice.

· The Lord's promise to His people...

The word is very near you, in your mouth
and in your heart, that you may do it.
DEUTERONOMY 30:14

With God in prayer...

·Find a portion of Psalm 119 (which is all about God's word) and pray through the words to make them your own.

Because His Word is your life...

What is the next Scripture verse or passage you will memorize? Choose it now, and start memorizing it today.

Your own reflections... personal application... personal prayer points...

THE PATTERN FOR PRAYER

When Jesus gave us the model prayer known as the Lord's Prayer, He said, "In this manner, therefore, pray" (Matthew 6:9). Notice He *didn't* say, "Here's a prayer to bring out when you're really in trouble."

In fact, Jesus didn't even instruct us necessarily to pray these words verbatim. Rather, He told us to pray "in this manner"—according to this pattern, along these lines. He gave us a structure for prayer.

> Lord, teach us to pray.
> Luke 11:1

If we were to design such a model prayer ourselves, it might go something like this: "Father in heaven, give me this day my daily bread." We like to cut to the chase in telling God what we want.

But Jesus said we should first focus on God's big concerns: "Our Father in heaven, hallowed be Your name. Your kingdom come. Your will be done on earth as it is in heaven" (Matthew 6:9–10).

Before we utter a word of personal need, we need to acknowledge that we're speaking to the Holy God—and we need to let that sink in. Before we bring our prayers before Him, we need to think about His holiness and glory and power. *Hallowed be Your name.*

And again, before a word of petition comes out of our mouths, we need to think and pray about His kingdom and authority and impact in this world, and all about His plans and purposes: *Your kingdom come. Your will be done on earth as it is in heaven.*

104

BECAUSE . . .

Why do you think it's so important for us to focus first on God's concerns when we pray?

By praying that way, we're essentially acknowledging that we have limited understanding, and we want God's will more than our own. This is how Jesus taught us to pray.

> The Lord's promise to His people...
>
> Your Father already knows your needs.
> He will give you all you need from day to day if you
> make the Kingdom of God your primary concern.
> JESUS, IN LUKE 12:30–31 NLT

With God in prayer...

Forgetting your own needs for a while, devote some time in prayer exclusively to God's concerns: honoring the holiness of His character, and seeking the full accomplishment of His purposes and His will.

Because God has plans and purposes...

As you focus your heart on God's kingdom and His will—what specific response does His Spirit bring to your mind? What does He want you to do *today?*

Your own reflections... personal application... personal prayer points...

Monday

OPEN HEART

I clearly remember when I was a new Christian and first began to discover this wonderful privilege we call prayer. I'd never prayed in my life. Oh sure, there were occasional cries to God for help when I was in trouble, but I hardly classify those are genuine prayer. I wasn't aware I could know God in such a way as to call on Him and listen to Him.

I also remember how nervous I was the first time I prayed with other Christians. With every word, I was convinced I was a failure in prayer.

Sometimes we think we don't know how to pray properly. We don't know how to phrase certain things. We wonder if we should be using King James English. We wonder if we should pray in a certain posture. But these aren't really significant issues.

In prayer, the really important thing is our heart. The great thing about prayer is that God looks primarily at our motive, our heart. Even if our prayers aren't perfectly structured, even if they aren't eloquent, as long as they come from a heart that's truly after God, they're pleasing to Him.

God always keeps up with the latest lingo, so don't worry about finding the right words. He'll never have trouble understanding what you mean. He knows what you're thinking.

So the main thing in prayer is simply to start praying. Just start where you are, and be honest with God.

> Keep on praying.
> 1 Thessalonians 5:17 NLT

Jesus once told His disciples a story "to illustrate their need for constant prayer and to show them that they must never give up" (Luke 18:1 NLT). So make it a habit to spend time in prayer, and never give up.

You can pray at home, or while waiting in a store's checkout line, or

BECAUSE

while you're stuck in traffic. Anywhere, anytime, you can pray—and God will hear.

> The Lord's promise to His people...
>
> You shall call, and the LORD will answer;
> you shall cry, and He will say, "Here I am."
> ISAIAH 58:9

With God in prayer...

Open your heart up before God. Do a heart examination in His presence, and talk with Him about everything you find.

Because God sees your heart...

Think about the people who are most on your heart, and take time today to pray intently for them.

Your own reflections... personal application... personal prayer points...

Tuesday

HEAR, THEN DO

If you've ever looked at yourself carefully in a magnifying mirror, you know what it's like to see every pore and imperfection in your face. But imagine walking away and immediately forgetting what you just saw. That would be difficult to do.

But according to James 1:23–24, this is what it's like when we fail to apply God's Word to our lives after we've heard it.

For if anyone is a hearer of the word and not a doer, he is like a man observing his natural face in a mirror; for he observes himself, goes away, and immediately forgets what kind of man he was.

James 1:23-24

As you're reading your Bible or listening to a message, maybe a certain truth really speaks to you. It's as though the Holy Spirit has said, "This is for you! Here's what you've been wondering about." It seems as though it's being directed to you and you alone.

Here's what it comes down to: What are you going to do about it?

Maybe after you thought, *That really spoke to me,* you also were thinking, *Now I need to do something about it.* But then you closed your Bible, or left the church service, and forgot about it. God has spoken to you through His Word, and you know you should *do* something in response, but you've basically ignored it.

This is what James is speaking of. We look at ourselves in the mirror of God's Word and realize we need to do something, but then we don't take action. But unless God's Word has made a change in our lives, then it hasn't really entered our lives.

We need to act on what we see in God's Word. It's not enough to just hear it. We also need to apply it.

108

> The Lord's promise to His people...
>
> Everyone then who hears these words of mine and
> does them will be like a wise man who built
> his house on the rock.
>
> JESUS, IN MATTHEW 7:24 ESV

With God in prayer...

Review with God the very last thing that you feel He spoke clearly to you about.

Because He expects your response to His words...

What will be your actual response to what God has most recently spoken to you about? What do you need to do or plan for *now?*

Your own reflections... personal application... personal prayer points...

GOD'S MOTIVATING LOVE

When the Pharisees brought a woman before Jesus and claimed that she'd been caught in the act of adultery (as we read in John 8), I wonder what was going through her mind.

The Bible does *not* say she was innocent of the charge laid against her by the Pharisees. So we may assume she was guilty. Trapped or not, she participated in this sin, and she bore responsibility for what she did.

As she watched these self-righteous, hypocritical, religious elitists in their attempt to have her put to death, she must have been amazed as Jesus told the Pharisees, "Let him who is without sin among you be the first to throw a stone at her" (John 8:7 ESV). While Jesus bent down to write in the sand, and her accusers drifted away one by one, maybe she thought, *What will He do to me now? He knows my worst secrets.*

What about your own **worst** secrets? What sins could be **legitimately** and publicly charged against **you**, just as the woman in John 8 was charged with adultery?

But I'm confident that when she looked into His eyes, she did not see condemnation. I believe she saw real compassion when He said to her, "Neither do I condemn you; go and sin no more" (John 8:11)

Why *didn't* Jesus condemn her, knowing she was actually guilty? Because in a short time, He would personally take *upon Himself* that very condemnation for her sin—and for yours and mine.

When we realize how much God has done for us—how He has wiped our slates clean when we deserve judgment for what we've done—our reaction should be, "I want to serve a God like that." When God looks at us in our miserable, fallen state and says, "I don't condemn you; now go and sin no more," we should *want* to live a godly life. We should *want* to please Him, not because we're bound to or we're afraid of righteous retribution, but because the love of God motivates us.

> The Lord's promise to His people…
>
> God did not send His Son into the world to condemn the world, but that the world through Him might be saved.
>
> JOHN 3:17

With God in prayer…

Give your fullest thanksgiving to God for this fact: "There is therefore now no condemnation to those who are in Christ Jesus" (Romans 8:1).

Because you are free from God's condemnation…

Record in writing (perhaps in the front of your Bible) your full recognition of the motivation and inspiration that's truly yours in light of the Lord's saving *love*. As the Scripture says, "We love Him because He first loved us" (1 John 4:19).

Your own reflections… personal application… personal prayer points…

Thursday

GO, AND SIN NO MORE

When Jesus spoke to the woman whom the Pharisees had caught in adultery and brought before Him, His words were full of promise—for us as well as for this woman.

We see first that *our sins can be forgiven and put behind us*. In speaking to this adulterous woman, Jesus never mentioned her sinful past. He didn't drag out the details. Instead He pronounced her free of divine condemnation: "Neither do I condemn you" (John 8:11).

This same freedom from God's condemnation is ours simply by faith in Jesus Christ. "He who believes in Him is not condemned" (John 3:18). Through faith in Christ, your sins no longer block your way to God. By coming to Christ in repentance and faith, it means "that your sins may be blotted out, so that times of refreshing may come from the presence of the Lord" (Acts 3:19).

> Your sins are **forgiven** you for His name's sake.
>
> 1 John 2:12

In the Lord's words to this woman in John 8, we also see how *we have new power to overcome our sin*. Jesus concluded His words to her by saying simply, "Go and sin no more." He would never have asked her to do something impossible. He wasn't saying she should be perfect; rather, He was telling her essentially to no longer live in a lifestyle of sin. In the same way, we no longer have to be under the control of sin. We can be free from it.

Does some sin have you in its grip right now? I want you to know that Jesus Christ can set you free. But you need to ask Him for His help. You need to take practical steps to distance yourself from your sin.

"Go and sin no more." This is what we need to do…because it's what we *can* do.

The Lord's promise to His people…

Therefore if the Son makes you free, you shall be free indeed.
JESUS, IN JOHN 8:36

With God in prayer...

Talk with God about any sin that may have you in its grip right now. And hear His empowering words to you: "Go and sin no more."

Because He frees you from your sin...

What practical step or steps must you take right now to distance yourself from any sin that has overpowered you in the past?

Your own reflections... personal application... personal prayer points...

Friday

A LIFE WORTH LIVING

Sometimes people think Christians live the most boring lives imaginable. But nothing could be further from the truth.

A true walk with Jesus Christ is life's grandest adventure, as you discover God's will for you and then walk in it. The truly happy life is a holy life—a life lived for God. Jesus not only promised us life beyond the grave, but He certainly promised us a dimension of life on this earth that's worth living when He said, "I have come that they may have life, and that they may have it more abundantly" (John 10:10).

> Are you convinced that holiness equals true happiness?
> Why or why not?

There are two ways we can live our lives—the right way or the wrong way. There are two paths we can take—the narrow path that leads to life or the broad way that leads to destruction. There are two foundations we can build on—the rock or sinking sand. The result is that we can either live a happy and holy life, or a miserable and unholy life.

When most people think of a life dedicated to God, they envision something full of misery and rules and regulations. The picture most unbelievers have of a Christian is one of gloom and boredom.

But when you know God and you realize the Bible isn't a mere book, but God's living Word to each of us, it takes on a whole new meaning. When you realize prayer isn't just going through some ritual, but it's communicating with the all-powerful, all-knowing, all-loving God who is interested in you, that means a lot. That's something the world doesn't have. There's nothing like it out there.

114

BECAUSE . . .

I am overwhelmed with joy in the Lord my God!
For he has dressed me with the clothing of salvation
and draped me in a robe of righteousness.

Isaiah 61:10 NLT

When you truly come to know God, you realize the Christian life is the greatest life there is.

> The Lord's promise to His people...
> All who receive God's wonderful, gracious gift of righteousness will live in triumph over sin and death through this one man, Jesus Christ.
> ROMANS 5:17 NLT

With God in prayer...

Thank Him for the degree of excitement and fulfillment He has given you in life.

Because the Christian life is the greatest there is...

What does "abundant life" really mean to you?

Your own reflections... personal application... personal prayer points...

Weekend

INSIDE OUT

People make changes in their lives for many reasons. Often it's when they face a crisis in life. It might be a heart attack. It might be the loss of a spouse through death or divorce. It might be some other crisis that hits them, and they begin to evaluate their priorities and take stock of their lives. They determine to make changes.

But often the same people who vow to change end up going back to their old ways. We often hear of celebrities going through drug rehabilitation treatment. We hear about the great changes they've made. They tell their stories on television and write books about it. But a short while later, we read that they've gone back to their old ways. Why? Because they've made outward changes in their lives, but haven't gotten to the root of their problem—which is the absence of God in their lives.

Jesus warned the Pharisees, "First wash the inside of the cup, and then the outside will become clean, too" (Matthew 23:26 NLT). Jesus wanted them to know that we're missing it when we concentrate only on the outward. We must first take care of the inward.

You try to look like upright people outwardly, but inside your hearts are filled with hypocrisy and lawlessness.

Jesus, in Matthew 23:28 NLT

The clear mandate given to the church from the lips of Jesus Himself was to go into this world and preach the gospel (Mark 16:15), because when people truly find Him, it will change their lifestyle. If, as believers, we allow other things to detract us from this calling to take the gospel into the world, then we're also missing it.

As Jesus said, if we wash the inside first, the outside gets clean, too. The *inside* is where we must focus our efforts.

> The Lord's promise to His people...
>
> God knows your hearts.
>
> JESUS, IN LUKE 16:15

With God in prayer...

Again today, offer thanksgiving to God for the cross of Jesus Christ, and how, for you and every human being, it solves our greatest problem—the problem of sin.

Because we're called to take His gospel into the world...

Who must you take the gospel to at once?

Your own reflections... personal application... personal prayer points...

THE KEY TO HOLINESS

Sadly, there are many believers today who live with a misconception that they must *do* something to earn God's approval and a righteous standing before Him. When they've had a good week and have been reading in their Bibles or doing certain good deeds for the Lord, they feel God must be pleased. But when they've had a spiritually tough week—when they've failed, when they've sinned—they think God can't be pleased with them.

After a discouraging week like that, they sometimes even conclude that they might as well not go to church or read the Bible. *Why bother?* they think. *God is so disappointed with me. It would be hypocritical for me to do anything spiritual.*

All the while, they fail to realize that they have God's unconditional favor and love regardless of what they do. His unconditional love is not a license to sin, however; rather, it's an incentive to respond to Him in love.

If, as believers, we can truly take hold of what this means—if we can understand that it isn't a license to live as we please—then it should be an incentive for us to serve the Lord, love Him, and show gratitude toward the One who loves us unconditionally, even while knowing us for what we are. An understanding of this truth can revolutionize our lives.

> Jesus Christ...gave Himself for us, that He might **redeem** us from every lawless deed and purify for Himself His own special people, zealous for **good** works.
> Titus 2:13-14

In some people's estimation, salvation comes from holy living—which to them means only keeping rules and regulations. But *true* holy living is something we are incapable of accomplishing, and therefore such an attempt can never bring our salvation.

True holy living is the *product* of our salvation in Christ. If you're truly saved, it will result in changes in your lifestyle.

> The Lord's promise to His people...
>
> Now may the God of peace make you holy in every way, and may your whole spirit and soul and body be kept blameless until that day when our Lord Jesus Christ comes again. God, who calls you, is faithful; he will do this.
>
> 1 THESSALONIANS 5:23–24 NLT

With God in prayer...

Thank the Lord for what He has done to save and sanctify you. Ask Him to show you how He wants to bring more holiness into your actions and attitudes.

Because He saved you to make you holy...

Because of the reality of your salvation, what holy actions is God calling you to carry out today?

Your own reflections... personal application... personal prayer points...

Tuesday

YOU DON'T NEED TO PRAY ABOUT IT

God speaks to us primarily through His Word, the Bible. So there are certain areas in which we don't need to pray for God's direction.

You need never walk up to me and ask, "Would you pray with me about murdering someone?" No, I won't pray with you about that, because I don't need to. God says in His Word, "You shall not murder" (Exodus 20:13).

Nor should you ever say, "Pray with me, because I'm thinking about having an affair and leaving my wife." No, I won't, because the Bible says, "You shall not commit adultery" (Exodus 20:14). You don't need prayer to find clear direction about this; you simply need to obey what God already says is right.

Are you prayerfully seeking how to escape certain responsibilities to your family? Or how to cheat someone financially and get away with it? Or how to "get back" at someone who offended you?

Don't bother. Just follow what the Bible clearly says is right and honorable in all these areas.

He has shown you, O man, what is good;
and what does the LORD require of you but to do justly,
to love mercy, and to walk humbly with your God?
Micah 6:8

What does the LORD your God require of you, but to fear
the LORD your God, to walk in all His ways and to love Him,
to serve the LORD your God with all your heart and
with all your soul, and to keep the commandments of the LORD
and His statutes which I command you today for your good?
Deuteronomy 10:12-13

For the grace of God has been revealed, bringing **salvation** to all people. And we are instructed to **turn** from godless living and sinful pleasures. We should live in this evil world with self-control, right conduct, and **devotion** to God.

Titus 2:11-12 NLT

There are many, many issues in our lives that we don't need to pray about, because in all these areas God has clearly shown us His active will for us in His Word.

The Lord's promise to His people...

"Be just and fair to all," says the LORD.
"Do what is right and good, for I am coming soon to rescue you.
Blessed are those who are careful to do this."

ISAIAH 56:1–2 NLT

With God in prayer...

Express your gratitude to God for how fully He speaks to us through the Bible on the daily issues of our lives.

Because God so clearly instructs us...

What has God shown you recently in His Word that you have failed to act upon? Act on it today.

Your own reflections... personal application... personal prayer points...

Wednesday

NO WORRIES

Have you ever been gripped by worry? I have. Sometimes I think I worry now more than at any other time in my life.

But worry just isn't a good thing for us. It isn't productive. It doesn't help.

In fact, it really hurts. Medical research has proven that worry is physically harmful to you. It can actually affect your central nervous system and make you less resistant to disease. Worry also can affect your digestive organs and your heart. Experts report that excessive worry can even shorten the human life.

You might be constantly worrying about whether something bad could happen to you—getting involved in an accident, for example, or contracting a terrible disease. But the irony is that even if such a thing never happened to you, you could actually shorten your life just by worrying about it too much.

> Therefore do not **worry** about tomorrow,
> for tomorrow will worry about itself.
> Each day has enough **trouble** of its own.
> Jesus, in Matthew 6:34 NIV

Are you someone who's gripped by worry right now? It has been said that worry is the advanced interest you pay on troubles that seldom come.

When we're tempted to worry, God says, "Do not be anxious about anything, but in everything, by prayer and petition, with thanksgiving, present your requests to God. And the peace of God, which transcends all understanding, will guard your hearts and your minds in Christ

Jesus" (Philippians 4:6–7 NIV). Isn't that a wonderful promise? Instead of worrying, the Bible tells us to bring our requests to God, and His peace will keep our hearts and minds. So the next time you want to worry, the next time you're gripped by anxiety, pray about it.

> The Lord's promise to His people...
>
> Cast your burden on the LORD, and He shall sustain you.
> PSALM 55:22

With God in prayer...

If there's any cloud of anxiety hanging over your head, no matter how slight, talk fully and honestly about this with God. He is more than willing to listen and help you. "So let us come boldly to the throne of our gracious God. There we will receive his mercy, and we will find grace to help us when we need it." (Hebrews 4:16 NLT).

Because He has the answer to our anxiety...

Make a list of the kinds of things you're most likely to worry about (as you look back on the patterns of your life). Even if these things aren't troubling you at the moment, bring the full list before God and ask for His help in averting any oppressive anxiety attacks about them in the future.

Your own reflections... personal application... personal prayer points...

Thursday

BEWARE OF BACKSLIDING

I've been a Christian now for a number of decades, and I can tell you with absolute assurance that there's no such thing as a spiritual plateau. You'll never arrive at a place in which you suddenly are above problems, above trials, and incapable of falling into sin. There is no super-spiritual state on this earth in which you'll no longer grapple with temptation. There is no level of Christian living you'll reach in this life that will somehow guarantee you're above it all.

No, our Christian life on earth is one of unending growth and constant change, and this transformation will continue until our lives come to an end here, and we meet the Lord in heaven.

But consider this: The moment you cease to progress as a Christian is the moment the process of backsliding potentially begins. When you cease to go forward, it's only a matter of time until you start going backward, and yes, even backsliding.

The word *backsliding* may seem kind of extreme, but did you know you can attend church every Sunday and still be a backslider? It's always a matter of what's happening in our hearts.

Your **backslidings** will rebuke you. Know therefore and see that it is an evil and bitter thing that you have **forsaken** the LORD your God.

Jeremiah 2:19

Falling away and backsliding is something we as Christians need to be constantly alert to, because the Bible warns that in these last days, an apostasy—a falling away from the faith—will take place: "Now the Spirit expressly says that in latter times some will depart from the faith, giving heed to deceiving spirits and doctrines of demons" (1 Timothy 4:1).

So keep your guard up—because if you're not moving forward as a Christian, you'll be going backwards. It's either one or the other.

> The Lord's promise to His people...
>
> My eyes are ever toward the LORD,
> for He shall pluck my feet out of the net.
> PSALM 25:15

With God in prayer...

Ask God to help you be alert and forewarned to any backsliding tendencies in your life.

Because there are no plateaus...

What kind of "backsliding" pressure have you sensed in your life? How have you responded? What should you do today to ensure forward progress instead of backsliding?

Your own reflections... personal application... personal prayer points...

THE WRONG TIME FOR JOY?

Have you ever gone through a tough time and someone has tried to comfort you with a greeting-card type slogan such as, "When life gives you lemons, make lemonade," or "Don't worry. Be happy"? How about that old favorite, "When the going gets tough, the tough get going"?

I don't know about you, but this approach doesn't comfort me. In fact, hearing things like that tends to make me even *more* miserable.

Yet James, who was writing to people who were suffering, told them this: "My brethren, count it all joy when you fall into various trials" (James 1:2). Now, what kind of counsel is that to give to those who are suffering? Was James advocating a sort of mind-over-matter method of coping? Was he encouraging these afflicted people to engage in possibility thinking or positive thinking?

Not at all.

Let's understand: James wasn't saying we should be experiencing an overwhelming emotion of happiness during times of hardship. Nor was he demanding that we actually enjoy the trials in our lives. He wasn't saying trials are joyful, because they're not. They're hard. They can be extremely tough. In fact, the Bible tells us (in reference to the tough trials that God brings into our lives to train and shape us), "For the moment *all* discipline seems *painful* rather than pleasant" (Hebrews 12:11 ESV).

My brethren, count it all JOY when you fall into various trials, knowing that the testing of your faith produces patience.

James 1:2-3

What James wants us to see is that we need to make a deliberate choice to experience joy. Why? Because those trials are accomplishing something in our lives—"the testing of your faith produces patience" (James 1:3).

So we can rejoice that God is in control of all circumstances (including *painful* circumstances) in the life of the Christian. We can rejoice in the fact that the word *oops* is not in God's vocabulary.

Isn't that great to know? God is in control.

The Lord's promise to His people...

In his kindness God called you to his eternal glory by means of Jesus Christ. After you have suffered a little while, he will restore, support, and strengthen you, and he will place you on a firm foundation.
1 PETER 5:10 NLT

With God in prayer...

Rejoice in the fact that God makes no mistakes in what He allows into your life.

Because God is in control...

How can you more *quickly* "count it all joy" when you face painful circumstances?

Your own reflections... personal application... personal prayer points...

SWIM UPSTREAM

"Just go with the flow," people say. But I'd rather not—because any dead fish can float downstream, but it takes a live fish to swim upstream.

If we just go with the flow and do what everyone else does, we may end up wasting our life and facing a certain judgment. Or we can go *against* the flow—by choosing the narrow way that leads to Christ.

True rebellion in our day is following Jesus Christ. If you want to be a real rebel, then say you believe in a God who sent His Son to die on the cross for you, and that trusting in Jesus Christ as your Savior and Lord is the way to find forgiveness of sins. And mention also that you believe God has given us His standards in the Bible—not to make our lives miserable, but to make our lives full.

> Enter by the narrow gate; for wide is the gate and broad is the way that leads to destruction, and there are many who go in by it. Because narrow is the gate and difficult is the way which leads to life, and there are few who find it.
>
> Jesus, in Matthew 7:13-14

Statements like these will make you a rebel in our culture and society today. Yet this is the narrow way—and it's the good way. Just as the Lord God says, "Stand in the ways and see, and ask for the old paths, where the good way is, and walk in it; then you will find rest for your souls" (Jeremiah 6:16).

The other option is the broad way. It isn't a hard road to walk. No rules. No regulations. Just go with the flow. The problem is that it leads to destruction. "There is a way that seems right to a man," the Bible says, "but its end is the way of death" (Proverbs 14:12).

God has given us the right way to live. It's the narrow way that leads to life.

> The Lord's promise to His people...
>
> He who loses his life for My sake will find it.
> JESUS, IN MATTHEW 10:39

With God in prayer...

Talk with your Savior about your desire to swim upstream, instead of drifting downstream, merely going with the flow.

Because the narrow way is the good way...

What aspects of the "broad way," the world's way, are most attractive and appealing to you? Are you holding on to some of them? Let go where you need to let go, and turn and walk the other way—the narrow way with Jesus that leads to life.

Your own reflections... personal application... personal prayer points...

BECOMING NEW—AND STAYING NEW

Scripture is full of descriptions of the believer's new spiritual life.

God promises He'll give us *a new heart*. He says, "I will give you a new heart and put a new spirit within you" (Ezekiel 36:26).

God also gives us *a new song*. David wrote, "He has put a new song in my mouth—praise to our God" (Psalm 40:3).

> Oh, sing to the LORD a new song! For He has done **marvelous** things; His right hand and His **holy** arm have gained Him the victory.
>
> Psalm 98:1

The Bible also promises us *a new self.* We're taught "to put off your old self, which belongs to your former manner of life and is corrupt through deceitful desires, and to be renewed in the spirit of your minds, and *to put on the new self,* created after the likeness of God in true righteousness and holiness" (Ephesians 4:22–24 ESV).

> That is why we **never** give up.
> Though our bodies are dying,
> our spirits are being **renewed** every day.
>
> 2 Corinthians 4:16 NLT

As believers, our spiritual lives are new, but we still have the capacity to sin. And though we have this capacity for sinning, the tyranny and penalty of sin in our lives has been broken.

However, sin's potential hasn't been fully removed, because we have two natures within that are constantly at battle—a new nature and an

BECAUSE . . .

old nature. As you know, it's very easy to sin. It comes naturally to us. But the new nature *doesn't* come naturally; it comes *super*naturally. These two natures are battling each other, and every day you determine which nature you're going to build up. Which will prevail? The one you build up the most. Every time you obey God and resist sin, you're building up the new nature.

> The Lord's promise to His people...
>
> The unfailing love of the LORD never ends!...
> His mercies begin afresh each day.
> LAMENTATIONS 3:22–23 NLT

With God in prayer...

God makes newness fully available to you today, and even surrounds you with newness. Do you see it? Thank Him for what you see.

Because He's the God of newness...

What "oldness" in your life do you need to let go of today?

I heard the story of an old man who compared his new and old nature to two dogs that were constantly fighting. He said he always knew ahead of time which dog would win. When asked how, he responded with a twinkle in his eye: "The one I feed the most!"

When you take time to 'feed' your new nature—to build yourself up spiritually—that's the best thing you can do to prevail in the never-ending conflict between right and wrong. How can you feed your new nature today?

Your own reflections... personal application... personal prayer points...

WHEN YOU WANT GOD TO USE YOU

What can we do to prepare for God's leading and calling in our lives?

We read in 1 Kings of a time when the prophet Elijah called the man Elishah to join him in the Lord's service. And what was Elisha doing at the time? Was he walking around saying, "I wonder if God will *ever* do anything in my life?" No. He was busy. He was plowing a field.

> So Elijah went and **found** Elisha son of Shaphat plowing a field with a team of oxen.... Elijah went over to him and threw his **cloak** across his shoulders and walked away again.
>
> 1 Kings 19:19 NLT

You'll find this pattern throughout Scripture. The people God uses are people who are *faithful in whatever He has put before them*. The people God uses in big things are those who are faithful in little things.

A lot of people think that one day in the future they would like to perhaps dedicate their lives to Christian service. They say, "I would like to go to another country and maybe become a missionary." That's great—but how about serving the Lord where you are right now? Do you think some mystical thing will happen the moment you step onto foreign soil? Seize the opportunities around you *today*.

> What fears or **worries** do you have about stepping into a new area of service to the Lord? How can you **overcome** those fears and worries?

If you want to go to a foreign land where people speak a different language, I know of such a place. The people indigenous to this region are small of stature and hard to understand. They try your patience. They're called kids, and the mission field is called Sunday school.

When we're busy looking for distant opportunities, we might miss the ones that are right in front of us. Are you serving the Lord right now with what He has called you to do? If so, be faithful in that. Hang in there. Do it well. Do it as unto the Lord. He sees you, and He'll one day reward you openly.

> The Lord's promise to His people...
>
> A faithful man will abound with blessings.
> PROVERBS 28:20

With God in prayer...

Ask God to make clear to you the ministry and evangelism opportunities He is bringing your way.

Because God will show you...

What are the ministry and evangelism opportunities that you should seize *now* and faithfully pursue?

Your own reflections... personal application... personal prayer points...

THE COST OF COMMITMENT

When the prophet Elijah draped his mantle (his outer robe) on Elisha's shoulders, it was a symbolic gesture that said, "I'm passing on my calling to you." From the account of this incident in 1 Kings 19, we discover a few things about Elisha.

First, we know he was a relatively wealthy man and came from an affluent home. The Bible says he had twelve yoke of oxen, and in those days, owning even one pair of oxen meant you were well off. Having twelve pair would indicate that Elijah must have owned a considerable acreage. So, for Elisha to leave this behind to follow Elijah was not an easy choice.

> So Elisha...arose and **followed** Elijah, and became his servant.
>
> 1 Kings 19:21

This calling was not an invitation to a leisurely life on easy street. The prophet Elijah's life had been a hard one. He had many enemies. He had people who hated him, most notably, Queen Jezebel. For Elisha to follow Elijah would mean he would have the same enemies. The same people who hated Elijah would now hate him.

Many people are surprised to find that the Christian life isn't a playground, but a battleground. The day you decide to follow Jesus Christ, you begin to face opposition from the devil. He doesn't want you to grow spiritually. He doesn't want you to move forward. So, he'll use every trick up his sleeve to try and pull you back.

We must recognize that to follow Christ means there's a price to pay. We may lose some friends. We may have to give up a few things. It may be difficult at times. But beyond any doubt, it's worth the cost.

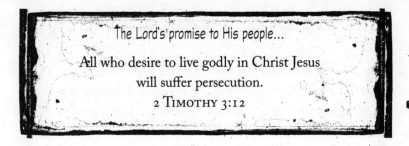

The Lord's promise to His people...

All who desire to live godly in Christ Jesus
will suffer persecution.
2 TIMOTHY 3:12

With God in prayer...

Ask God to strengthen you, enabling you to endure whatever hardships
and sacrifices He will bring next into your life.

Because following God is worth the cost...

What are the most significant difficulties and sacrifices you have
experienced in life since becoming a Christian? What has God taught
you through these hardships?

Your own reflections... personal application... personal prayer points...

THE DEVIL MADE ME DO IT(?)

Some people like to blame the devil every time they fall into sin. They'll say something to this effect: "Satan got me good the other day. I was just minding my own business, walking with the Lord, and the devil just grabbed me."

Please! If you're a Christian, the devil cannot "just grab you." You are under God's protection.

This protection from God doesn't mean you won't be tempted by Satan. It doesn't mean he won't try to hassle you. But he can't just pick you off at will. He has to have God's permission for any form of temptation to even reach you.

> God is **faithful**. He will keep the temptation from becoming so strong that you can't stand up against it. When you are **tempted**, he will show you a **way** out so that you will not give in to it.
>
> 1 Corinthians 10:13 NLT

However, some people will put themselves unnecessarily in the way of temptation, and then blame God when they fall. But don't blame God when you foolishly put yourself into a vulnerable place and then get tempted. When that happens, you really have no one to blame but yourself.

God knows what you can take when it comes to temptation. He won't give you more than you can handle. When my son Jonathan was younger and we would carry in the groceries, I would give him things like a roll of paper towels and a half gallon of milk to take into the house. "This is too heavy," he would say.

BECAUSE

"Buddy, you can do it," I would tell him. I knew he had more strength than he realized.

It's often that way with us. We may think, "This is too much. I can't handle it." But God knows what we can endure. He knows what we can take. He knows our weaknesses. And He won't ever let us face more than we can handle.

> The Lord's promise to His people...
>
> He gives power to the weak, and to those who
> have no might He increases strength.
> ISAIAH 40:29

With God in prayer...

Give praise to God for His true faithfulness in protecting you from more temptation than you could ever handle.

Because God is faithful...

Think back to recent situations where you've faced temptation. What are the ways of escape that God provided for you? What can you do to be more alert to these ways of escape from temptation situations in the future?

Your own reflections... personal application... personal prayer points...

Friday

GOD'S POP QUIZZES

When Paul and Silas were imprisoned for preaching the gospel, the Bible says they sang praises to God at midnight. They had previously been stripped of their clothing and beaten with rods; their backs were likely scarred and bleeding. Now their feet were in stocks as they sat in a dungeon. Do you think they *felt* like singing praises at the moment?

I doubt it. But they were able to realize God was in control. It was not mind over matter; it was faith over circumstances. It was not rejoicing in what they were going through; it was rejoicing in the fact that God had not abandoned them. He hadn't forgotten about them. He would accomplish His work.

> But at midnight Paul and Silas were praying and singing hymns to God, and the prisoners were listening to them.
> Acts 16:25

One of the first thoughts coming to mind when we go through difficulties is *Why is this happening to me?* We wonder what we've done to deserve such a thing.

> Have you ever asked God, "Why is this happening to me?"

It's important to know that God *does* have lessons He wants to teach us during these trials. Of course, I would like to learn what God is trying to teach so I can move on. I don't want to repeat any courses, if possible.

Remember in school when the teacher announced a pop quiz? If you were like me, you felt a sinking sensation when such an announcement was made. (That's because I'd rarely done my homework.) Well, I have some news for you: God gives pop quizzes too. Often He doesn't announce them. We may think we're really learning and growing in the Christian life. So God will give us a trial to see if we're learning as much as we think we are. That testing will reveal how much faith we really have.

> The Lord's promise to His people...
>
> The fire will test each one's work.
> 1 CORINTHIANS 3:13

With God in prayer...

Think of the Christian brothers and sisters you know who are currently going through severe trials, and offer up your prayers for them.

Because God is faithful to teach and train you...

What are the most important lessons God has recently taught you through trials? Be fully aware and appreciative of them.

Your own reflections... personal application... personal prayer points...

NOT HOME YET

A century ago, a missionary couple who had served for many years in Africa were returning to the United States. Leaving Africa with broken health and no pension, they felt defeated, discouraged, and somewhat afraid.

As it turned out, former President Teddy Roosevelt was traveling on the same ship, returning from a hunting expedition. Of course, it caused a great commotion aboard ship as everyone tried to catch a glimpse of Roosevelt.

With all the attention shown to the former president, a sense of injustice swept over the missionary, who was traveling in obscurity. After all, he and his wife had given their lives in service to the Lord for all those years in Africa; why should a man returning from a mere hunting trip receive such vastly greater attention than they did?

When the ship arrived in New York City, awaiting them was a cheering throng, a brass band, and the mayor—all to welcome the former president. But no one in that vast crowd was there to welcome the missionary couple.

"It isn't fair," the missionary told his wife, fully expressing the resentment he felt in comparing Roosevelt's reception with their own.

Then his wife told him, "Why don't you just go and tell that to the Lord?"

A short while later, the missionary was smiling. "What happened?" his wife asked. "You look different."

He answered, "Well, I told the Lord how bitter I felt to see the president welcomed home that way, but no one here to greet us. Then it seemed as though the Lord put His hand on my shoulder and said, 'Son, you aren't home yet.'"

Many who seem to be **important** now will be the least important then, and those who are considered **least** here will be the **greatest** then.

Jesus, in Matthew 19:30 NLT

God sees everything you do for Him, and He will not fail to bless you. But remember: We aren't home yet.

• The Lord's promise to His people...

God is not unfair. He will not forget how hard you have worked for him and how you have shown your love to him by caring for other Christians, as you still do.

HEBREWS 6:10 NLT

With God in prayer...

In what kind of circumstances have you been most tempted to think that God is unfair? Talk with God about this, and renew your hope in His future eternal blessings.

Because you're not home yet...

What labor and service for the Lord are you engaged in now? Renew your commitment to God to keep serving faithfully, without discouragement over any obscurity or perceived lack of results.

Your own reflections... personal application... personal prayer points...

WHY PRAY?

Why should we pray?

Among many reasons, there's a devil. The Bible says, "Be sober, be vigilant; because your adversary the devil walks about like a roaring lion, seeking whom he may devour" (1 Peter 5:8).

The Bible teaches that we're engaged in a spiritual battle unlike any earthly conflict—"For we do not wrestle against flesh and blood, but against principalities, against powers, against the rulers of the darkness of this age, against spiritual hosts of wickedness in the heavenly places" (Ephesians 6:12).

God has given us prayer as a way of dealing with our satanic adversary. Through prayer, we can accomplish things in the supernatural realm.

> Prayer is God's appointed way for us to obtain the things we truly need and most deeply desire.

Another reason to pray is that it's God's appointed way for us to obtain things. The Bible says, "You do not have because you do not ask" (James 4:2). Of course, some have taken this idea to extremes: They teach that if there's anything you happen to want, just "name it and claim it" in the name of Jesus, and God will give it to you. They've misunderstood a wonderful promise of God regarding prayer, by neglecting sensitivity to God's holy will and character and intentions.

We also can go too far in the other direction and fail to receive all that God has for us, simply because we don't ask. You might be sick. Pray and ask God's healing touch on your body. Maybe you're in need of financial help. Pray. Maybe you wonder why certain things aren't happening in your life. Have you prayed about it? Have you taken it

142

before the throne of God and said, "Lord, here's a need in my life. I need your help"?

God *is* interested in you, and He wants to answer your prayers. But He wants your full participation in the process.

The Lord's promise to His people...

If you then, being evil, know how to give good gifts to your children, how much more will your Father who is in heaven give good things to those who ask Him!

JESUS, IN MATTHEW 7:11

With God in prayer...

Give appropriate thanks to God for His faithful commitment to hear your requests.

Because we wrestle against dark powers...

As you think about the spiritual warfare we're called to, what specific response does God's Holy Spirit bring to your mind? What does He want you to do *today*?

Your own reflections... personal application... personal prayer points...

WAITING FOR ANSWERS

An interesting story in the Old Testament book of Daniel offers us a rare, behind-the-scenes look at what happens when we pray.

The Bible tells us that Daniel was praying, and his prayer reached heaven. God heard Daniel's prayer and dispatched an angel with a special message for Daniel.

But for twenty-one days, this angelic messenger was prevented from reaching Daniel, because of spiritual warfare with a powerful demon spirit. Not until the messenger received help from Michael the archangel was he able to overcome this dark enemy and to deliver God's special message to Daniel.

Despite this three-week delay, the angel assured Daniel of God's responsiveness to his prayer: "Do not fear, Daniel, for from the first day that you set your heart to understand, and to humble yourself before your God, your words were heard; and I have come because of your words" (Daniel 10:12).

Sometimes when God doesn't answer our prayers as quickly as we would like Him to, we think He's letting us down. We need to understand that delays are not denials.

How hard is it for you to be "kept in the dark" when your **prayers** go **unanswered**? Does your faith in God need to be strengthened?

When we pray and don't see an answer as quickly as we would like, there may be a spiritual battle going on behind the scenes. It can happen when you've been praying for someone to come to know the Lord, or for God to heal you, or for God to open up doors of opportunity for your service to Him.

Don't give up. Don't be discouraged. Keep praying.

Jesus taught us to keep asking, keep seeking, and keep knocking, and the door would be opened (Matthew 7:7–8).

So be persistent. And watch what God will do.

The Lord's promise to His people...

Wait on the LORD; be of good courage,
and He shall strengthen your heart; wait, I say, on the LORD!
PSALM 27:14

With God in prayer...

What delays are you currently experiencing in receiving answers to your prayers? Talk openly with your heavenly Father about these, and communicate to Him your trust in His timing.

Because God's timing is perfect...

What is the best way to combine patient trust in God with faithful persistence in prayer? What should this look like in your life?

Your own reflections... personal application... personal prayer points...

Wednesday

GOD'S UNFAILING LOVE

The Bible tells us that God actually *is* love. It's not merely that God *has* love or that He's loving. The Bible actually says God *is* love.

> God is love.
> 1 John 4:8

Today, people's view of love is mostly a Hollywood version that's very shallow. It's probably closer to lust than anything else. Hollywood's version of love basically says, "I love you as long as you're lovable." Or, "I love you as long as you're beautiful." Then this: "But the moment you cease to interest me, I'll trade you in on the new model. I'll move on to another relationship."

In contrast, God's love is unchanging and unconditional. It's consistent. It's inexhaustible. He *always* loves us. He loves us when we're sitting in church with smiles on our faces and a Bible in our laps, but He also loves us when we're failing and when we're sinning. Though God is displeased by our sin, He still loves us, no matter what we do. So we need to remember this about God.

> May the Lord **direct** your **hearts** into the love of God.
> 2 Thessalonians 3:5

But I want you to know something about sin: Sin will cost you. Sin is very expensive. Many advertisements today will urge us to "Buy now, pay later." We love that, because it almost seems as though we're getting something free. But payday *will* come—with interest.

In the same way, the devil says, "Play now. And you never have to pay." But sin will *always* cost. Adam's sin cost him paradise. David's sin cost him his family and his reputation. Samson's sin ultimately cost him his life.

What is your sin costing you? Whatever it is, let the love of God draw you back to Him and away from your sin.

The Lord's promise to His people...

For the LORD is good; his steadfast love endures forever,
and his faithfulness to all generations.
PSALM 100:5 ESV

With God in prayer...

Rejoice in His love today.

Because God is love...

How is your life demonstrating to those around you that God is love?

Your own reflections... personal application... personal prayer points...

Thursday

A PASSION FOR THE LOST

General William Booth, founder of the Salvation Army, once said that his desire, had it been possible, would be to dangle his evangelism trainees over hell for twenty-four hours. That way, they could see the reality that awaits those who don't know Jesus Christ.

That wouldn't have been necessary for the apostle Paul, who spoke of his love and burning passion for unbelievers.

> My heart's desire and prayer to God for Israel is that they may be saved.
> Romans 10:1

Paul had something essential for effective evangelism—a God-given burden for those who did not know Jesus Christ. In his case, the burden was for his own people, the Jews. Paul cared deeply for them. It was a caring that burned inside him. He wrote, "My heart is filled with bitter sorrow and unending grief for my people, my Jewish brothers and sisters" (Romans 9:2–3 NLT).

Then Paul adds a truly amazing statement. He says, in essence: "If it were possible, I would give up my hope of eternal life so that others who do not know could come to faith" (Romans 9:3) That's a pretty dramatic declaration.

I think this statement of Paul's is there for us in Scripture so we don't become so obsessed with our own struggles and spiritual growth that we forget about people who need to know Christ.

As believers, you and I have a responsibility to those outside the faith. If God's love is really working in our lives, it should motivate us to help these people who are eternally lost.

Do you have a God-given burden for those who don't know Jesus Christ? If you don't, do you want such a burden?

If you pray that God will give you this burden, be careful. The results could be life-changing! You may be surprised at how quickly He answers you.

> The Lord's promise to His people...
>
> The Lord...does not want anyone to perish.
>
> 2 PETER 3:9 NLT

With God in prayer...

Ask God to give you a burden and passion for those who are spiritually lost.

Because there is salvation in Jesus Christ...

What are the most strategic ways you can interact with nonbelievers to promote opportunities to share with them the good news of Jesus Christ?

Your own reflections... personal application... personal prayer points...

Friday

SPREADING OUR WINGS

When a mother eagle teaches her eaglet to fly, she will unceremoniously kick it out of the nest—which may be ninety feet or more above the ground.

The little bird will fall and almost hit the ground—then suddenly get snatched by the mother eagle who has swooped down just in time. She'll put the eaglet back into the nest, then kick it out again. She'll do this again and again. Finally, that little eaglet starts using its wings.

This may seem like a cruel teaching method, but that's how eagles learn to fly.

Sometimes God will kick you out of your nest. You might be in a comfort zone in which everything is going the way you want it to. Then the Lord will say, "It's time for you to grow up a little more. It's time for you to stretch your faith. It's time for you to spread your wings."

> When your faith is **tested**, your endurance has a chance to grow.
> So let it grow, for when your endurance is **fully** developed,
> you will be **strong** in character and ready for anything.
> James 1:3-4 NLT

God will test you because He wants you to mature. He wants you to develop a walk with Him that isn't based on your fluctuating emotions, but on your commitment to Him as you learn to walk by faith.

> Grow in the **grace** and knowledge of our Lord and
> Savior Jesus Christ.
> 2 Peter 3:18

James 1:2 doesn't say, "Count it all joy *if* you fall into various trials." Rather, it says, "Count it all joy *when* you fall into various trials." It's only a matter of time until the next trial will come along.

Trials aren't an option. We will all be tested. The question is, when these tests come, will you pass or fail?

The Lord's promise to His people...

By standing firm, you will win your souls.
JESUS, IN LUKE 21:19 NLT

With God in prayer...

Ask God to make you stronger, in reliance on Him, for facing the trials that are coming your way soon.

Because God will test you...

What "nests" has God recently kicked you out of? Have you started using your "wings"?

Your own reflections... personal application... personal prayer points...

TABLE IN THE SHADE

It amazes me how flippant and casual people can be when they consider God's offer of forgiveness, as though they had all the time and resources in the world. They believe they can invent the rules as they go, nonchalantly picking and choosing what appeals to them on a celestial salad bar of life. They'll take a small amount of Christianity (but hold the guilt, because they're on a guilt-free diet), add a little Hinduism, then maybe a side of Buddhism. Finally, they season it all with a good sprinkling of New Age spices.

But here's the real picture: We're in the middle of a hot desert, dehydrated and starving. There's no food or water in sight, and we have no resources to purchase them anyway.

Suddenly, God appears. He sets out a beautiful table in the shade with the finest, freshest gourmet offerings available, and He invites us to come and dine.

And it's all free. The price for this sumptuous feast has already been paid. All we have to do is take a seat and feast away.

There are no other options. It's simple: Eat and live—or don't eat and die.

What makes us think that we can **escape** if we are indifferent to this great **salvation** that was announced by the Lord Jesus himself?

Hebrews 2:3 NLT

God offered only one way for us to be forgiven of our sins when He came to this earth, walked among us, went to the cross, and died in our place. We aren't doing God a favor by casually mulling over His offer. God is, in fact, doing *us* an incredible favor by offering it in the first place.

Every human being should be running to Him to receive His offer of forgiveness before it's too late.

And once we receive it—we should never stop giving thanks.

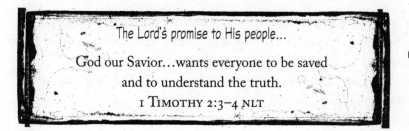

The Lord's promise to His people...

God our Savior...wants everyone to be saved
and to understand the truth.
1 TIMOTHY 2:3–4 NLT

With God in prayer...

Express your gratitude for the feast God has provided in order to save your life.

Because God has offered you life...

What does it mean personally to you to partake of the spiritual feast God has provided for you? Are you taking enough time for this today?

Your own reflections... personal application... personal prayer points...

Monday

THE SOURCE OF YOUR TEMPTATIONS

We all know what it's like to be tempted. Unfortunately, we also know what it's like to *give in* to temptation. We all want to learn how to better resist the temptation that comes our way.

Where does temptation come from? I can assure you that it *doesn't* come from God, as the Bible makes clear.

> Let no one say when he is **tempted**, "I am tempted by God"; for God cannot be tempted by **evil**, nor does He Himself tempt anyone.
>
> James 1:13

In our own temptation, *we* play the key role. For the devil to succeed in tempting us, we must listen, yield to, and (most importantly) desire what he has to offer. Where there's no desire, there's no temptation.

> But each one is tempted when he is drawn away by his own **desires** and enticed.
>
> James 1:14

The devil will use various types of bait to help people surrender to their desires. When I went on a fishing trip to Alaska, we used different kinds of bait and lures to attract the fish. In the same way, the devil will use different tactics to pull us into his snare. The devil also works with two close allies in our temptation—the world and the flesh. These three—the world, the flesh, and the devil—are a deadly trio.

By the term *world*, I mean a world system that's hostile to God. I'm not speaking of the planet Earth, but a way of thinking or a mentality.

That's why the Bible tells in Romans 12:2, "Do not be conformed to this world," or as one translation puts it, "Don't let the world around you squeeze you into its own mold" (PHILLIPS).

And the term *flesh* refers to our natural sinful desires, our weak and corrupted human nature.

So the three enemies we face are the world, the flesh, and the devil.

> The Lord's promise to His people...
>
> The Lord is faithful; he will make you strong
> and guard you from the evil one.
>
> 2 THESSALONIANS 3:3 NLT

With God in prayer...

Give thanks to God for the way He is strengthening you against yielding to temptation.

Because you are the key source of your own temptations...

What specific desires do you need to watch most carefully in your life, to keep them from leading you into sin?

Your own reflections... personal application... personal prayer points...

Tuesday

TRANSFORMING TRIALS

God never tests us without a purpose or a reason. When He allows us to go through trials, He always has a long-term goal in mind—to conform us into the image of Jesus Christ.

> For whom He foreknew, He also **predestined** to be conformed to the **image** of His Son, that He might be the firstborn among many brethren.
>
> Romans 8:29

Fortunately there are many times in our lives when we can look back on a trial we've been through, and see good things that have happened in our lives as a result. At times like these, we're reminded of Romans 8:28: "And we know that all things work together for good to those who love God, to those who are the called according to His purpose." A lot of things that make no sense at the time will work out in the end.

A classic example of this is the Old Testament story of Joseph. One day, as a youth, he was on top of the world; the next day he was literally at the bottom of a pit, and his own brothers sold him into slavery.

Decades later, Joseph, with the advantage of twenty-twenty hindsight, was able to look back and say to his brothers who betrayed him, "You meant evil against me; but God meant it for good" (Genesis 50:20).

I've seen a lot of things happen in my own life that I didn't understand at the time. But after a few years passed, I was able to look back and see why the Lord allowed them.

However, sometimes we never quite understand a trial's good purpose. There will be tough things you endure in life that will not have a convenient explanation. There will be some unanswered questions.

What unanswered questions do you have
about the trials God has allowed in your life?

BECAUSE...

157

But on that final day, when we stand before God, we know all our questions will be answered, all our problems resolved. Then we'll truly grasp how God's wise love was at work in *all* our trials.

> The Lord's promise to His people...
>
> I...will refine them as silver is refined, and test them as gold is tested. They will call on My name, and I will answer them. I will say, "This is My people"; and each one will say, "The Lord is my God."
>
> ZECHARIAH 13:9

With God in prayer...

Praise Him for how wise and loving He is in controlling the trials He brings into your life.

Because God has perfect reasons for testing you...

How are you seeing your life and character being conformed to the image of Jesus Christ because of the hardships you've known?

Your own reflections... personal application... personal prayer points...

Wednesday

NO TAIL CHASING

During a visit to the home of friends who lived in the mountains, I noticed a dog chasing his tail. I watched as he got closer and closer to the edge of a little hill, but because he was so preoccupied with his tail, he didn't notice, and rolled down the hill to the bottom. He climbed back up and started chasing his tail again.

On a return visit a few months later, I didn't see this dog anywhere. So I asked, "Where's the dog that chases his tail?"

"He caught it," they told me. "He bit it off and died."

Like that dog, we can chase after empty pursuits, but once we get them, we're more miserable than ever. We've been created to know God, and nothing is going to satisfy us except Him.

> God...has planted eternity in the human heart.
> Ecclesiastes 3:11 NLT

God wants you to be a happy person, but before that can happen, He must first make you into a forgiven person. When you find His forgiveness, you'll find happiness.

Do you want to find true happiness? Then you need to be poor in spirit; you need to see yourself as you really are. The Bible says, "All have sinned and fall short of the glory of God" (Romans 3:23). Every one of us falls miserably short of God's standards.

But in our misery, God has reached down to us. Jesus walked this earth as God in human form, went to the cross, and died for our sins— paying the penalty *we* should have paid.

When we turn from our sin, acknowledge our condition, and let Him be our Savior and Lord, we can truly find the ultimate happiness we're seeking in life.

> The Lord's promise to His people...
>
> Blessed is the one whose transgression is forgiven,
> whose sin is covered.
>
> PSALM 32:1 ESV

With God in prayer...

"O LORD, I am your servant...and you have freed me from my bonds!
I will offer you a sacrifice of thanksgiving and call on the name of the
LORD" (Psalm 116:16–17 NLT). In prayer, offer to the Lord a worthy
"sacrifice of thanksgiving" for the forgiveness and freedom and fullness of
life that He has provided you through the death of His Son, Jesus Christ.

Because He saved you from an empty life...

Ask yourself these questions (and discuss them with others as well):
What have you found to give true happiness in your life? And how does
it depend on God?

Your own reflections... personal application... personal prayer points...

Thursday

NEVER SATISFIED

"Whoever drinks of this water will thirst again" (John 4:13)—Jesus spoke those words to a woman who was trying to fill the void in her life with men. Jesus and the woman were standing beside a well in Samaria, but He wasn't just referring to the water in the well. Rather, He was speaking of the pursuits of life.

You can take that statement Jesus made and apply it to whatever you're depending on for fulfillment in life. You can apply it to a career: "Whoever drinks of this water will thirst again." You can apply it to a relationship: "Whoever drinks of this water will thirst again." You can apply it to possessions: "Whoever drinks of this water will thirst again." You can apply it to *anything* that might take the place of God in your life. It won't really satisfy; you'll always thirst again.

In what ways are you finding yourself repeatedly unsatisfied?

No matter what we obtain, no matter what we achieve, we always want more. Scripture says, "Hell and Destruction are never full; so the eyes of man are never satisfied" (Proverbs 27:20). *Never satisfied*—that's how life goes when one's body, mind, and spirit are not yielded to God. Life becomes a vicious circle, because the natural heart of a person is never content.

This can even affect our prayer lives. James says, "You ask and do not receive, because you ask amiss, that you may spend it on your pleasures." (4:3). It comes down to our motives in prayer.

BECAUSE . . . .

They cried to the LORD, but he refused to answer them.

Psalm 18:41 NLT

It's very important to know what motivates us, because when God listens to our prayers, He looks into our hearts. And He knows what we're really asking for; He knows what we really desire.

> The Lord's promise to His people...
>
> Everything belongs to you...the whole world and life and death; the present and the future. Everything belongs to you, and you belong to Christ, and Christ belongs to God.
>
> 1 CORINTHIANS 3:21–23 NLT

With God in prayer...

Talk with Him about your true and deepest desires.

Because Christ satisfies our true thirst...

What are you doing to drink your fill of Christ today?

Your own reflections... personal application... personal prayer points...

Friday

THE PURSUIT OF PLEASURE

According to the Bible, one of the signs of the "last days" is that people will be "lovers of pleasure rather than lovers of God" (2 Timothy 3:1, 4).

That's an accurate assessment of our culture today. We're a pleasure-mad society. We want to be constantly entertained, titillated, and thrilled. We want constant activity taking place in our lives. We're entertaining ourselves to death.

What part does the pursuit of pleasure play in your life?

The Bible doesn't say that pleasure in and of itself is necessarily wrong. Many pleasures have been given to us by God Himself. The Bible assures us that there are "pleasures forevermore" as well as "fullness of joy" in God's presence (Psalm 16:11). The Bible speaks also of a level of happiness that can be experienced only by the man or woman who's walking with God. "No good thing will He withhold from those who walk uprightly" (Psalm 84:11). This reminds us that there's nothing God tells us to avoid that is good. If He withholds it from us, it's only because it will harm us.

*Your goodness is so great! You have stored up great **blessings** for those who honor you. You have done so much for those who come to you for **protection**, blessing them before the watching world.*
Psalm 31:19 NLT

162

BECAUSE . . . .

But there are also sinful pleasures—which are *never* acceptable for the child of God. We must accept this by faith, because there'll be times when certain things in the world look so appealing, so exciting. They'll be tantalizing. But if God says no to something, then not having it is for our own well-being. He'll never hold back anything from us that's good.

Yet when pleasure becomes the focus of our lives, we'll be miserable, because it rarely brings what we're searching for.

163

> The Lord's promise to His people...
>
> How precious is your unfailing love, O God! All humanity finds shelter in the shadow of your wings. You feed them from the abundance of your own house, letting them drink from your rivers of delight.
> PSALM 36:7–8 NLT

With God in prayer...

Give thanks to God for some of the many pleasures and blessings He has brought into your life. Be specific!

Because all the best pleasures are in God's presence...

Are there any ways in which your life is focused on pleasures rather than on God Himself, the source of all true pleasures?

Your own reflections... personal application... personal prayer points...

Weekend

FAITHFUL IN THE LITTLE THINGS

When I was a young Christian attending Calvary Chapel in Costa Mesa, California, I would listen to Pastor Chuck Smith and some of the other pastors there and think, "That's what *I* want to do; I want to serve the Lord like that. I want to speak."

I'd been a believer for three or four months when I went to see Pastor Chuck one afternoon. I sat down in his office and said, "I've been listening to you speak. I want you to know that I want to be used by God. Whatever you want me to do around here, I would be happy to do it."

I was kind of hoping he would answer something like this: "Greg, why don't you teach for me Sunday morning?" Instead, he suggested that I talk to Romaine, another pastor at Calvary Chapel. Romaine was a former drill sergeant in the Marine Corps.

So I went to Romaine's office and told him, "I want to be used by God."

"You do?"

I said, "Yes I do. I want to serve the Lord."

"That's great," Romaine said. He pointed outside his window. There was a pepper tree which appeared to have only one function—to drop leaves on church property.

"See that tree? See that broom? Start sweeping."

> Unless you are faithful in small matters,
> you won't be faithful in large ones.
> Jesus, in Luke 16:10 NLT

I went out and started sweeping under that tree. I would sweep it clean, but only a few minutes later, there seemed to be about a couple hundred more leaves there. I would sweep it up again. Then two hundred more leaves. It's all I did for months in serving the Lord at that church—just sweeping under that tree and doing little things around the church property. But it was good. They were testing my faithfulness.

Do you want to be used by God? Then be faithful in the little things.

Remember: You're never too small for God to use; only too big!

The Lord's promise to His people...

Who is a faithful, sensible servant...? If the master returns and finds that the servant has done a good job, there will be a reward. I assure you, the master will put that servant in charge of all he owns.

JESUS, IN MATTHEW 24:45-47 NLT

With God in prayer...

Let Him know how much you truly want to serve Him, and thank Him for every little opportunity He gives you to do this.

Because God wants to build up your faithfulness...

What "little things" has God given you as a test of your faithfulness? How well are you doing? What needs to change?

Your own reflections... personal application... personal prayer points...

Monday

FRIENDSHIP WITH THE WORLD

When you see the term *the world* in the Bible, it usually isn't speaking of the physical planet Earth. This term generally speaks of a system, a mentality, or a way of thinking that's controlled by the god of this world, Satan. That's true in James 4:4, where we're warned about "friendship with the world."

> Do you not know that friendship with the world is enmity with God? Whoever therefore wants to be a friend of the world makes himself an enemy of God.
>
> James 4:4

This kind of "friendship" has to do with love in the sense of strong emotional attachment—to love, to have an affection for, or even to kiss. James is warning us about a deep, affectionate love we might have for the world.

The world has a value system, and it's all around us. It's in the movies, on the Internet, on TV and the radio, and in magazines and newspapers and books. It's taught as dogma in our classrooms. We're expected to march in step with what we're told is the right thing to believe.

It's a value system entrenched in moral relativism. As a result, everyone's afraid of declaring certain things as right or wrong. *Tolerance* has become the watchword of the day. Don't judge other people, we're told.

This, of course, poses a problem for the Bible-believing Christian, because we don't subscribe to the theory of moral relativism. We believe there *is* absolute truth, there *is* right versus wrong, there *is* good versus evil.

If you were of the world, the world would love its own.
Yet because you are not of the world,
but I chose you out of the world, therefore the world hates you.

Jesus, in John 15:19

So what are we to do when we're surrounded by this mentality, this system that's so contrary to what the Word of God teaches? The only way to counteract this world's message is to fill your heart and mind with the things of God.

The Lord's promise to His people...

For whatever is born of God overcomes the world.
And this is the victory that has overcome the world—our faith.

1 JOHN 5:4

With God in prayer...

Give thanks to God for solid truth—for the true absolutes that He reveals to us in His Word.

Because God is your truest Friend...

How can you fill your heart and mind today with God Himself?

Your own reflections... personal application... personal prayer points...

Tuesday

HOW TO DRAW NEAR TO GOD

There's only one way to draw near to God, and that's to first recognize we're sinners. We need to recognize that only the shed blood of Christ—and never our own worthiness—will give us access to God's throne.

> Draw **near** to God and He will draw near to **you**.
>
> James 4:8

You see, the devil will lie to you and say, "You're not worthy to pray. What makes you think God would hear *you* after what you've done today?"

The devil is clever. He'll tempt you to do something wrong, and then if you do it, he'll condemn you for it. He'll insist, "You can't go to God now." And you'll believe it, being overwhelmed by your own unworthiness.

But does this mean that when you're doing well spiritually, you're suddenly *worthy?* Does it mean you're worthy if you've read your Bible today, read in a devotional book (like this one), listened to Christian radio all day long, and prayed over your meals?

I have news for you: You *aren't* worthy. You aren't worthy when you're doing well spiritually, nor are you worthy when you're doing terrible spiritually. Your access to God isn't based on worthiness. It's based on the shed blood of Christ.

> You were NEVER worthy enough to approach God...
>
> not even on your **best** day!

BECAUSE . . .

It's good to get into God's Word, to pray, to fellowship with other believers, and to share your faith; these are what should be happening in the life of a committed believer. But these things don't give you access to God.

My access to God is always on the basis of the blood of Christ. So when I've sinned, when I've failed—that's the time I should really make the effort to draw near to God. And when you draw near to God, He will draw near to you.

The Lord's promise to His people...

Yes, I have loved you with an everlasting love; therefore with loving-kindness have I drawn you and continued My faithfulness to you.

JEREMIAH 31:3 AMP

With God in prayer...

Give thanks for the true worthiness you can enjoy before God through Christ.

Because God is near...

What can you do to keep from drifting away from God today in your thoughts and attitudes?

Your own reflections... personal application... personal prayer points...

Wednesday

A VANISHING VAPOR

Here's an interesting question for you: What really *is* your life?

You do not know what **tomorrow** will bring. What is your life?
For you are a mist that appears for a little time and then vanishes.

James 4:14 ESV

When James asks this question (in James 4:14), it isn't a philosophical inquiry. Rather, James is reminding us of the shortness of human life.

This theme is echoed throughout Scripture: "Now my days are swifter than a runner; they flee away" (Job 9:25); "Man who is born of woman is of few days and full of trouble. He comes forth like a flower and fades away" (Job 14:1–2).

James compares our lives to a mist or a vapor that appears and then vanishes. That illustration really puts our lives into perspective!

James was addressing his words to Christians who seemed to be taking credit where credit wasn't due. They were boasting of their ability to make money and be successful. In the process, they were forgetting all about God. That's a dangerous thing to do, because God will not share His glory with another.

James tells us that instead of boasting like that, "You ought to say, 'If the Lord wills, we shall live and do this or that'" (James 4:15). James wasn't condemning the person who makes plans for the future. Rather, he was criticizing the person who makes those plans with no thought whatsoever of God's will.

In your own planning for the future, how do you work in an
acknowledgement of God's will?

BECAUSE...

171

There's nothing wrong with making plans, and we don't need to say out loud "If the Lord wills," every time we plan something. We can make our plans. We can state our purposes. We can have our agenda. But we also need to recognize God may have *other* plans in store for us, and we must be willing to accept that.

The Lord's promise to His people...

If the LORD delights in a man's way, he makes his steps firm; though he stumble, he will not fall, for the LORD upholds him with his hand.

PSALM 37:23–24 NIV

With God in prayer...

Review with Him the most important plans and expectations you currently have in your life, and yield yourself to God's overriding will in each area.

And you may want to add this little P.S. to your prayers: "Lord, if what I've prayed is somehow outside of Your will for me, just disregard it. Not my will, but Yours be done."

Because your life is only a vapor...

Have you honestly accepted and faced how short your life on earth truly is?

Your own reflections... personal application... personal prayer points...

NO CHASING SARDINES

Some years ago, three hundred whales were found marooned on a beach. Scientists speculated that the whales had been chasing small fish and had become trapped in shallow water when the tide went out.

Now that's an amazing thing. By chasing sardines, these gigantic creatures were led to their doom.

Many people waste their lives chasing sardines, so to speak. They major on the minors and have no clear focus or objective in mind.

In your life, are there any "**sardines**" you're chasing?

But God tells us what should be the primary goal of every Christian. If we can get our priorities straight in this area, everything else will come together. In fact, if we can get these two principles operative in our lives, then all the commandments of God will become a natural outflow of our commitment to Him.

What are these principles? First, "You must love the Lord your God with all your heart, all your soul, and all your mind"; Jesus said this is "the first and greatest commandment." Then He added, "A second is equally important: 'Love your neighbor as yourself'" (Matthew 22:37–39 NLT).

We know we **love** God's children if we love God and **obey** his commandments.

1 John 5:2 NLT

BECAUSE . . . .

When Jesus spoke these words, He was identifying what should be the primary focus of every person. Essentially, He was saying that *love is the basis for all obedience.* If you really love God, you'll naturally want to do the things that please Him.

It has been said, "If you aim at nothing, you're bound to hit it." What's *your* highest priority in life? What are your goals? We all channel our energies and passions and thoughts toward something in life. What is it for you?

> The Lord's promise to His people...
>
> Love never fails.
> 1 CORINTHIANS 13:8

With God in prayer...

If you haven't already done this, evaluate with God your true priorities in life.

Because love is the basis for everything else...

How can you practically demonstrate *today* your love for God and your love for other people?

Your own reflections... personal application... personal prayer points...

Friday

MOVING GOD'S WAY

Sometimes when people are facing a tough decision or difficult circumstances, I hear them describe their prayers about it in these words: "I've been wrestling with God." My first thought always is, *I hope you lost!*

If you've been trying to bend God your way, that's a problem. Prayer isn't trying to move God your way; it's moving yourself His way.

In fact, I'm glad God hasn't said yes to every prayer I've ever prayed. When I look back on some things I've prayed for, I realize that if the Lord would have allowed them, they could have destroyed me. They weren't the right things or the right situations. That's why God graciously and lovingly said no.

In John 15:7, Jesus gives us an incredible promise regarding answered prayer: "If you abide in Me, and My words abide in you, you will ask what you desire, and it shall be done for you." The Lord's meaning there could also be translated this way: "If you maintain a living communion with Me, and My words are at home with you, I command you to ask at once for yourself whatever your heart desires, and it will be yours."

When I read a promise like that, I gravitate immediately toward the part that says I can ask whatever my heart desires and it will be mine. But before that promise comes this condition: "If you maintain a living communion with Me, and My words are at home with you."

I will **delight** myself in Your commandments, which I **love**.

Psalm 119:47

If this is happening in your life, you're going to want what God wants. If you're maintaining a living communion with God and His words are at home in your heart, then your outlook, your desires—and in time, your prayers—*will* change.

BECAUSE

> The Lord's promise to His people...
>
> Delight yourself also in the LORD,
> and He shall give you the desires of your heart.
> PSALM 37:4

With God in prayer...

In living communion with the Lord, express honestly to Him how much you want what *He* wants in your life.

Because He wants to fulfill your desires...

Make a list of the most significant things you want in life, and evaluate them honestly according to their conformity to God's will.

(And if you want to know more about prayer and its place in the believer's life, you may want to take a look at a book I've written called *Wrestling with God,* published by Multnomah.)

Your own reflections... personal application... personal prayer points...

THREE ENEMY STRATEGIES

You can take any temptation you've ever faced in your life, and it will fall under one of the three categories mentioned in 1 John 2:16—"the lust of the flesh, the lust of the eyes, and the pride of life."

The lust of the flesh primarily speaks of the gratification of our physical desires. It isn't wrong to desire food or sleep or to have a sexual drive. All these can be satisfied within God's natural order (the sexual drive being satisfied exclusively within the bonds of marriage). But it's possible to let any of these things *control* our lives. Instead of simply eating to live, you can find yourself living to eat. Instead of just wanting to rest, you can become lazy. So the lust of the flesh is physical temptation.

> Put on the Lord Jesus Christ, and make no **provision** for the flesh, to fulfill its lusts.
> Romans 13:14

The lust of the eyes is a little different. This speaks primarily of mental sins (such as immoral "fantasies" in your mind), or the things that gratify our wrong perceptions or our obsession with appearances.

> Hell and Destruction are never **full**;
> so the **eyes** of man are never satisfied.
> Proverbs 27:20

Last, there's *the pride of life,* which is more subtle than lust of the flesh or lust of the eyes. The clever strategy of the pride of life is that you can pursue knowledge to better yourself, or even seek to be a relatively

religious person, yet be overwhelmingly selfish and self-centered about it.
These are strategies that the enemy uses in each of our lives.

> You **boast** [falsely] in your presumption and your self-conceit.
> All such boasting is **wrong.**
>
> James 4:16 AMP

It's good to know about these things, because the Bible says we shouldn't be ignorant of the devil's schemes and strategies and deceits (see 2 Corinthians 2:11). Victor Hugo once said that a good general must penetrate his enemy's brain. So know what your enemy is up to.

> The Lord's promise to His people...
>
> You are strong with God's word living in your hearts,
> and you have won your battle with Satan.
>
> 1 JOHN 2:14 NLT

With God in prayer...

Pray this request from the prayer pattern that Jesus taught us: "And do not lead us into temptation, but deliver us from the evil one" (Matthew 6:13).

Because Christ has overcome the evil one...

"For this purpose the Son of God was manifested, that He might destroy the works of the devil" (1 John 3:8). Since Christ has defeated Satan, how can you practically rely on Christ's victory *today?*

Your own reflections... personal application... personal prayer points...

GIVING HIM THE GLORY

When we become proud of our abilities and insist that we can accomplish whatever we put our minds to, we're making a big mistake.

> You boast in your **arrogance**. All such boasting is evil.
>
> James 4:16

The Bible tells us it's the Lord who gives us the ability to do what we do. It's the Lord who gives us the very breath we draw in our lungs. It's the Lord who has given us our heartbeats. It's the Lord who gives us the ability to earn a living. Everything we have is a gift from God. We must never forget that.

> You were bought at a price; therefore **glorify** God in your body and in your spirit, which are God's.
>
> 1 Corinthians 6:20

> Use your whole body as a **tool** to do what is right for the glory of God.
>
> Romans 6:13 NLT

In the Old Testament we read of how one day King Nebuchadnezzar stepped out on his royal balcony and surveyed this ancient wonder known as Babylon. He stood there, took in all of its splendor, and said, "Is not this great Babylon, that I have built for a royal dwelling by my mighty power and for the honor of my majesty?" (Daniel 4:30).

The Bible says these words were still on his lips when a voice came

178

BECAUSE . . .

from heaven saying, "King Nebuchadnezzar, to you it is spoken: the kingdom has departed from you!" (Daniel 4:31). Judgment came swiftly upon him.

We never want to look at any success we've had—in a career, in ministry, in relationships, in athletics, in music, or in anything else—and say, "Look at what I've done. Look at what I've accomplished." It's the Lord who has given us this ability, and we should give Him the glory for whatever we've accomplished.

The Lord's promise to His people...

Unless the LORD builds a house, the work of the builders is useless.

PSALM 127:1 NLT

With God in prayer...

Confess any pride that you may be harboring about any success or accomplishments you have known.

Because all your abilities are from the Lord...

How can you consciously give more glory to God for the things He allows you to accomplish?

Your own reflections... personal application... personal prayer points...

NEEDING REMINDERS

A number of years ago, I received one of those dreaded notices in the mail. It was time for me to take my driving test again.

At the time I thought, *I've been driving every day for decades now, so I don't need to read the manual again.* When I showed up at the DMV for my appointment, I was handed a written test. Some of the questions stumped me a bit, but I thought I did reasonably well. After all, I was allowed to have three wrong answers and still pass the test, and I was sure I hadn't missed that many.

I took my test back to the DMV employee. I watched as she pulled out a red pen and, with great relish, began to check my test. She marked one wrong. Then two. Then three, four, five, six...

"You have to take the test again," she told me.

Eventually I passed the test—barely. It was a humiliating experience.

I had assumed I knew all the basics, but obviously I did not. I had to go back and read the manual. It reminded me that I don't necessarily know as much as I think I do.

There are things in life we forget. The place where that's critically true is in our spiritual lives.

> Beware that you do not **forget** the LORD your God by not **keeping** His commandments.
>
> Deuteronomy 8:11

That's one of the reasons Peter wrote his second epistle—to remind believers of basics that we so easily forget.

I will not be negligent to remind you always of these things,
though you know and are established in the present truth.
Yes, I think it is right...to stir you up by reminding you.

2 Peter 1:12-13

If we focus on the things we should never forget—and hold on tightly to them—then God says we'll "never stumble", and He'll allow us to enter "abundantly" into His kingdom (2 Peter 1:10–11).

The Lord's promise to His people...

Work hard to prove that you really are among those God has called and chosen. Doing this, you will never stumble or fall away. And God will open wide the gates of heaven for you to enter into the eternal Kingdom of our Lord and Savior Jesus Christ.

2 PETER 1:10–11 NLT

With God in prayer...

Express your gratitude to God for the needed reminders He faithfully brings into your life.

Because you need reminders...

What are the "basics" of the Christian life that you tend to lose sight of most easily? What should you do to hold on to them more tightly?

Your own reflections... personal application... personal prayer points...

Wednesday

TAKE IT PERSONALLY

When God revealed to the prophet Daniel that He would bring judgment on Israel, Scripture shows us how personally moved Daniel was as he considered this prophecy: "Then I set my face toward the Lord God to make request by prayer and supplications, with fasting, sackcloth, and ashes. And I prayed to the LORD my God, and *made confession*" (Daniel 9:3–4).

Daniel took it *personally*, and he communicated personally how sorry he was for his own sin.

As we think about the Lord's imminent return, we might say, "God will judge this world. He'll finally deal out the justice that's so desperately needed in our culture today." But when God points out what's wrong with our world spiritually, He doesn't point His finger at government or the media. He points His finger at His own people—at the church. In effect that means He points His finger at you and me, who as believers are part of His church.

Today when we look at what's spiritually and morally wrong in our culture, we're quick to place the blame on the White House, or Congress, or Hollywood, or the media establishment, or someone else.

But God says that when a nation is sick, it's because there's a problem with His church. God says the problem is with His people.

> If My people who are called by My name will **humble** themselves, and pray and seek My face, and turn from their wicked ways, then I will hear from heaven, and will **forgive** their sin and heal their land.
>
> 2 Chronicles 7:14

Here's what it comes down to: How should the fact that Christ is coming back affect *you*? Don't worry about the rest of the world. Don't even worry about the other Christians you know. How should it affect *you*?

> The Lord's promise to His people...
>
> For the time has come for judgment to
> begin at the house of God.
>
> 1 PETER 4:17

With God in prayer...

Humble yourself, and pray, and seek God's *face* (as He tells us to do in 2 Chronicles 7:14).

Because Christ is coming back to judge the world...

What should change in your life today because of your expectation of the Lord's return?

Your own reflections... personal application... personal prayer points...

Thursday

READY, EAGER, AND PATIENT

Remember how you felt as a child on Christmas Eve? If you were like me, you could hardly wait. You had a hard time getting to sleep. When morning came, you sprang out of bed. You were anxious to see what was waiting for you under the Christmas tree.

This kind of eager expectancy is the attitude that James refers to when he tells us, "Therefore be patient, brethren, until the coming of the Lord." (James 5:7). This kind of "patience" is *not* a passive resignation; it's *not* an attitude that says, "I guess He's coming one of these days. Whatever."

Rather, it's a prolonged, expectant, excited attitude as we look for the Lord's return. It's an attitude of readiness.

Yet some believers are not living this way. Instead, they're just biding their time. But God tells us we should be active as we await the return of Christ.

Be ready, for the Son of Man is coming at an hour you do not expect.
Jesus, in Matthew 24:44

God wants us to wake up to the urgency of the hour. He's telling us to be ready.

It is high time to awake out of sleep;
for now our salvation is nearer than when we first believed.
Romans 13:11

James compares this kind of eager waiting to the farmer who "waits for the precious fruit of the earth, waiting patiently for it until it receives the early and latter rain" (James 5:7). In Israel, the early rains will usually come in late October or early November. These will soften the hard-baked soil for plowing. The latter rains usually come in late April or May and are essential to the maturing of the crops. If a farmer were to rush out and harvest his crops before their time, he would destroy them. He has to wait.

And so do we.

> The Lord's promise to His people...
>
> When Christ who is our life appears,
> then you also will appear with Him in glory.
> COLOSSIANS 3:4

With God in prayer...

Honestly express to Him your level of expectancy and eagerness and excitement as you look for Christ to return.

Because the Lord is coming back...

How can you be a better "waiter" today—more expectant, more eager, more excited?

Your own reflections... personal application... personal prayer points...

Friday

SINLESSNESS

I had to laugh when I heard the story of two men who one day approached the legendary British preacher, C. H. Spurgeon, and told him, "Spurgeon, we have reached sinless perfection."

"Really?" he asked.

"Yes," they said, "We're absolutely perfect."

Spurgeon was holding a pitcher of water at the time, and he proceeded to pour it on their heads. When they began to react like any other sinners would, he found out just how perfect they were.

You see, the people who walk around claiming to have reached sinless perfection are victims of one of the most powerful yet subtle sins—pride. None of us will reach sinless perfection in this life. In all of human history, Christ alone has been sinless.

> If we say that we have no sin, we deceive ourselves, and the truth is not in us.
> 1 John 1:8

Granted, something dramatic happened when we received Christ. Before we were Christians, we were under the control and power of sin. We went along with whatever our sinful natures dictated. But in Christ we were changed. The Bible says we became new creations in Christ; old things passed away and everything became new (see 2 Corinthians 5:17).

But that isn't to say we still don't struggle with sin or that we'll have no lapses. When we fall, we can go at once to Christ for cleansing, according to His promise in 1 John 1:9.

However, if we're sinning habitually and persistently and without sincere confession, something's terribly wrong. If someone claims to be a Christian and yet continues consistently in certain sins, my question is

186

BECAUSE

whether that person has ever been truly converted. Some people wonder whether such a Christian ever could lose his or her salvation. I would suggest asking another question instead: Did he or she ever experience salvation to begin with?

> The Lord's promise to His people...
>
> If we confess our sins, He is faithful and just to forgive us our sins and to cleanse us from all unrighteousness.
>
> 1 JOHN 1:9

With God in prayer...

Acknowledge before God your sinfulness and your continual need for the blood of Christ to cleanse you from sin. Give thanks to Him that because of the cross, "We are no longer slaves to sin" (Romans 6:6 NLT).

Because Jesus Christ is our righteousness...

Step forward confidently in the freedom from sin that Jesus Christ has won for you. "Go and sin no more" (John 8:11).

Your own reflections... personal application... personal prayer points...

Weekend

MOVED TO ACTION

Biblical expositor Alexander McLaren once said, "You tell me the depth of a Christian's compassion, and I will tell you the measure of his usefulness."

How deep does your compassion go? God is looking for such people.

How does it affect you, knowing there are many people who don't know Christ, people who are basically on their way to a certain judgment? Does it move you? Until you're moved in the depths of your soul, you will not be moved to take any action.

Nehemiah was a man in a position of great influence and power as he served under the king. He wasn't a preacher or priest or scribe, but Nehemiah loved God.

One day, someone told him about the plight of the Jews and how Jerusalem was now lying in ruins. Nehemiah began to weep and pray, asking the Lord to show him how he should respond to this problem.

> And they said to me, "The survivors who are left from the captivity in the province are there in great distress and reproach. The wall of Jerusalem is also broken down, and its gates are burned with fire." So it was, when I heard these words, that I sat down and wept, and mourned for many days; I was fasting and praying before the God of heaven.
>
> Nehemiah 1:3-4

The devastation of Jerusalem had touched him, and he wanted to do something about it.

After his despair came determination; after his weeping came working. As he prayed, he devised a plan. Then that plan began to unfold.

Here are two essential ingredients for effectively sharing our faith:

One, it must start with a God-given burden, leading us to prayer. And two, we need to then go out and do something.

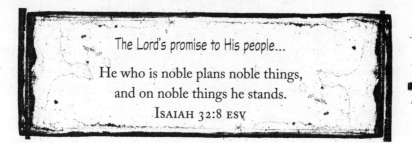

The Lord's promise to His people...

He who is noble plans noble things,
and on noble things he stands.

ISAIAH 32:8 ESV

With God in prayer...

Among the millions of unsaved people in this world, who can you specifically pray for today? How about a neighbor or family member who does not yet know the Lord?

Because God answers prayer...

What can you do now to reach the unbelievers you are praying for?

Your own reflections... personal application... personal prayer points...

AT THE RIGHT TIME

By nature, I'm an impatient person. I'm one of those guys who, when the pizza comes, doesn't wait for it to cool off. I start eating it immediately. Of course, I've burned the entire roof of my mouth that way. But I just can't seem to wait.

In this day and age when everything moves so fast, we don't need to wait for much of anything anymore. How did we ever make it without microwave ovens? Yet even these seem slow to me now.

At the grocery store, even if it's necessary for me to leave a few things behind, I'll try to get in the ten-items-or-less line. When I'm on the freeway, if one lane starts to move, even if it's just slightly faster than my lane, I'll move to the faster one. I just don't like to wait.

Yet the Lord tells us, "You must be patient as you wait for the Lord's return" (James 5:7 NLT).

> The Lord whom you **seek** will suddenly come to his temple;
> and the messenger of the covenant in whom you **delight**,
> behold, he is **coming**, says the LORD of hosts.
>
> Malachi 3:1 ESV

As we look at this world in which we live and the way our culture is changing, we may think, "Lord, hurry! Come back! Look at the way things are going."

But God has His own schedule. He won't be late. He won't be early. He'll be right on time.

Be **patient**. Establish your hearts, for the coming of the Lord is at hand.

James 5:8

When He came the first time, it was according to His perfect plan: "When the right time came, God sent his Son" (Galatians 4:4 NLT). I love that phrase, "when the right time came." At the appointed hour, Jesus Christ, the Son of God, fulfilled the Old Testament prophecies and was born in a manger in Bethlehem.

And when the time is just right, Jesus Christ, the Son of God, will return.

The Lord's promise to His people...

The day of the Lord will come as a thief in the night.

2 PETER 3:10

With God in prayer...

Thank the Lord *now* (just as you will in eternity) for His perfect timing regarding His return to earth.

Because Jesus Christ will come back...

Think with concentration about the Lord's return and what it should mean in your life. Should you make any changes in your current plans? Adjust any priorities?

Your own reflections... personal application... personal prayer points...

Tuesday

THE ROD AND THE STAFF

David speaks in Psalm 23 of two essential tools of a shepherd.

A *staff* is the long, crooked instrument a shepherd uses to pull in wayward sheep—and sheep are definitely wayward. They have a natural tendency to go astray and to get themselves into trouble. They also have a natural tendency to follow each other. If one sheep goes astray, the others will follow, even to their own death. Sheep are so compliant they'll follow what other sheep do regardless. So a shepherd must use his staff to pull the wayward sheep in.

The shepherd will use his *rod* to fight off intruders, such as wolves or lions. But sometimes the shepherd also uses the rod on his own sheep— his sweet, little sheep that he loves so much. Why? Because he would rather use the rod than see them dead. He would rather whack them in the leg than see them wander off into a predator's reach. For some stubborn sheep, the staff simply doesn't work. So the shepherd pulls out the rod and applies it.

> Your rod and Your staff, they **comfort** me.
>
> Psalm 23:4

The Bible says, "All we like sheep have gone astray; we have turned, every one, to his own way" (Isaiah 53:6). Because we have such a wayward, selfish tendency, the Lord will use the staff in our lives. When we go astray and do something we shouldn't do, the Holy Spirit convicts us. If we keep doing it, the Spirit convicts us again. If we keep on going, God will pull out the rod. *Wham!* Something dramatic happens. All of a sudden, the bottom drops out. It's the rod.

The rod isn't meant to destroy us, but to warn us of the danger of what we're doing. God uses the rod in our lives because He loves us.

The Lord's promise to His people...

For the Lamb who stands in front of the throne will be their
Shepherd. He will lead them to the springs of life-giving water.
And God will wipe away all their tears.
REVELATION 7:17 NLT

With God in prayer...

Express your gratefulness for the discipline God has recently brought into
your life.

Because God disciplines those He loves...

In your situation, how well is God's discipline working right now?

Your own reflections... personal application... personal prayer points...

WHEN WE'RE SUFFERING

If you're suffering, the Bible says the first course of action is to pray. "Is anyone among you suffering? Let him pray" (James 5:13). There's nothing wrong with asking God to remove your suffering.

When hardship comes, I'll pray and ask the Lord to remove it. But then I'll add, "Lord, if I've brought this on myself through some act of disobedience, or this is something You want to use to get my attention, please show me what it is so I can do what You want me to do."

There are also times when our suffering is not of our own doing, but something the Lord has allowed, as in the case of Job. During those times, we must wait on the Lord and trust He has a plan and purpose in mind.

In the day of my trouble I sought the Lord.
Psalm 77:2

The apostle Paul faced a great affliction. We don't know what it was exactly, but he described it as "a thorn in the flesh," and Paul prayed repeatedly for God to take it away: "Concerning this thing I pleaded with the Lord three times that it might depart from me" (2 Corinthians 12:7–8).

There are theories about the nature of his affliction, but all we know is that something was physically troubling the great apostle. He asked the Lord for deliverance, but God had something better planned for Paul.

God answered Paul's request in this way: "My grace is sufficient for you, for My strength is made perfect in weakness" (2 Corinthians 12:9). God continued to allow this suffering in Paul's life, as a demonstration of His own strength being perfected in Paul's weakness.

In spite of what you're going through, remember God is still in control. The word *oops* is not in His vocabulary.

> The Lord's promise to His people...
>
> Not that we are sufficient of ourselves to think of anything as being from ourselves, but our sufficiency is from God.
>
> 2 CORINTHIANS 3:5

With God in prayer...

Bring before Him any hardships you're experiencing now, and offer this request: "Lord, if I've brought this on myself through some act of disobedience, or this is something You want to use to get my attention, please show me what it is so I can do what You want me to do."

Because His grace is sufficient...

In your life, how can you see that God is allowing His strength to be perfected in your own weaknesses?

Your own reflections... personal application... personal prayer points...

Thursday

TEMPTATION'S TIMING

When does temptation come our way?

In a broad sense, it can come at any time. Often it comes after great times of blessing, after the Lord has done a wonderful work in your life.

> Immediately the Spirit drove Him into the wilderness.
> And He was there in the wilderness forty days, tempted by Satan...
>
> Mark 1:12-13

Remember how Jesus spent forty days and nights in the wilderness, where he was tested and tempted by Satan. When did this happen? It happened immediately after His baptism in the Jordan River, when the Spirit of God came upon Him in the form of a dove, and a voice came from heaven saying, "You are My beloved Son, in whom I am well pleased" (Mark 1:11). After the dove came the devil. After the blessing came the attack.

After times of great blessing in our own lives as well, the enemy will often show up, wanting to rob you of what God has done in your life. You may have experienced a time of the Holy Spirit's working in your heart, then suddenly you were plunged into a dark valley.

Maybe things have been going really well for you lately. Things are going well for your family, with your career, with your ministry, and with your personal walk with the Lord. That's good. Enjoy it—because the enemy will show up and try to rattle your cage. He'll attack you. He'll tempt you. It isn't a matter of "if"; it's a matter of "when."

So keep your guard up. The devil will wait for the opportune time to attack. The devil will be sizing you up. He'll be waiting for that moment when you're most vulnerable. And we're often the most vulnerable when we think we're the strongest.

> The Lord's promise to His people...
>
> He who is in you is greater than he who is in the world.
>
> 1 JOHN 4:4

With God in prayer...

Ask God to give you clear understanding of how you need to guard against temptation.

Because temptations will always come your way...

What have you found to be your most vulnerable times of being tempted to sin? How can you keep your guard up in such times?

Your own reflections... personal application... personal prayer points...

THE LAW THAT LIBERATES

One afternoon, a brightly colored little bird landed in my backyard. My German Shepherd wasn't far away, and I knew the moment he saw that bird, it would become an appetizer for him. So I went over to the bird and bent down. It was shaking, its feathers fluffed. When I held out my finger, the little bird hopped on. I walked into the house and said to my wife, "Cathe, look at this little bird." She turned around to see it perched stiffly on my finger.

"Where did you get that?"

"Our backyard."

"It must be someone's pet."

"Yeah, but I don't know who it belongs to."

My son Jonathan walked in just then, and seeing the bird, he told us about a girl down the street who said her bird had died.

A short while later, Jonathan had retrieved the bird's cage from the girl's home. We put the cage on our kitchen counter and opened its door, and I placed the bird inside.

The bird, which had stayed frozen on my finger all this time, suddenly came alive. He chirped and hopped from perch to perch. His feathers smoothed down. It was obvious he liked his new surroundings.

Then it dawned on me: What we saw as a means to contain this little bird was, from his standpoint, a means of security and protection. In his little bird-brain, he saw those cage bars not as a barrier to keep him in, but as a defense to keep my dog out!

In the same way, God gives us His laws and His standards in the Bible. While we might see them as restrictive, they are, in reality, our source of protection.

I will walk in freedom, for I have **devoted** myself to your commandments.

Psalm 119:45 NLT

That's why James calls it "the perfect law of liberty" (James 1:25).

> The Lord's promise to His people...
>
> Now the Lord is the Spirit; and where the Spirit of
> the Lord is, there is liberty.
>
> 2 CORINTHIANS 3:17

With God in prayer...

Talk with God about any area of life where you tend to feel restricted or in bondage.

Because the Word of God gives us freedom...

In what area of life do you sense God wanting to move you into more freedom? Fully apply His Word in this area, and begin today.

Your own reflections... personal application... personal prayer points...

WHO WILL GO?

God said in the presence of Isaiah, "Whom shall I send, and who will go for Us?"

Isaiah answered, "Here am I! Send me" (Isaiah 6:8).

In a sense, God is still asking this question. *Whom shall I send? Who will go for Us?*

What will be your answer? Will you go? Will you stand in the gap?

As God's Holy Spirit searches among us today, I wonder if He is finding men and women willing to stand in the gap. Willing to pray. Willing to be available. Willing to reach out to those who don't know Him.

> The kingdom of heaven is like a certain king who arranged a marriage for his son, and sent out his servants to call those who were invited to the wedding; and they were not willing to come.
>
> Jesus, in Matthew 22:2-3

A lot of Christians will say, "I'm too timid." They're afraid of this or that. But I think a lot of Christians don't really have a burden for those who don't know the Lord. I think if that burden is burning with enough passion, a believer will work through the obstacles and the fears.

That isn't to say we can't take time to first learn more about how to share our faith more effectively. But if the burden is really there, a believer will go out and do something with it.

The bottom line is that sharing our faith isn't really a big deal to many of us. This is why it's so important to have a God-given burden for unbelievers.

I would rather make every mistake possible in sharing my faith than to never share at all. At least I'll hopefully learn something from my mistakes. But when we do nothing for fear of being rejected or for fear we won't meet with resounding success, we're really missing what God has called us to do.

The Lord's promise to His people...

I am not ashamed of the gospel of Christ, for it is the power of God to salvation for everyone who believes.

ROMANS 1:16

With God in prayer...

Give thanks for the people who shared their faith with you, helping you to come to salvation.

Because God is asking, "Who will go?"...

What is your answer?

Your own reflections... personal application... personal prayer points...

PRAYING FOR HEALING

God has given us, as Christians, the promise of divine healing. In Isaiah 53:5, in a passage that prophesies of Jesus Christ, we read this: "And by His stripes we are healed." God can and will heal people today.

In James 5 we're given the scriptural pattern for this healing. If we're sick, we're to ask the elders of the church to pray for us:

> Is anyone among you sick? Let him call for the elders of the church, and let them pray over him, anointing him with oil in the name of the Lord. (James 5:14)

Although the Bible teaches that there are and were miracles of healings, it's interesting that nowhere in the Bible do we read of anyone having a ministry devoted to "faith-healing" or a "miracle ministry."

We do read, however, that everyone had a gospel-preaching ministry. Their calling was to proclaim God's Word, and the Lord at times would confirm that proclamation of His truth with signs that followed. It was never God's plan to put the *focus* on miracles or signs and wonders; the focus was always on Jesus Christ and on telling people how to believe.

> Praise the LORD, I tell myself, and never forget the **good** things he does for me. He **forgives** all my sins and heals all my diseases.
> Psalm 103:2-3 NLT

I don't think we should ever announce a "miracle service" to be held at a certain time and place. It's up to the Lord to choose where and when He will sovereignly do the miraculous or heal someone.

Believers should never follow signs and wonders; rather, signs and wonders should follow believers.

At the church where I pastor, we pray for people who are sick, and people often are healed. I'm so thankful the Lord still heals us today. We should ask for God's touch and healing. We're certainly given that option in Scripture, and we ought to exercise it. Sometimes God will heal. But other times, He won't.

Either way, we need to remember God always has a plan and purpose in mind, and we need to trust Him.

> The Lord's promise to His people...
>
> I am the LORD who heals you.
> EXODUS 15:26

With God in prayer...

Pray for the Lord's healing for those you know who are ill or injured.

Because the Lord is our healer...

What healing from God do you need now in your life? Go ahead and ask Him. "You do not have because you do not ask" (James 4:2).

Your own reflections... personal application... personal prayer points...

Tuesday

TEMPTATION'S TARGETS

Although temptation comes to everyone, the enemy often focuses his attacks on those who are young in the faith or on those who are making a difference in the kingdom.

You probably remember how the devil was there to tempt you after you became a Christian. One thing you most likely faced was a tendency to doubt your own salvation. Satan whispered in your ear, "So you think you're saved? You think Christ really came into your life? You only psyched yourself into this. It's a bunch of nonsense. What are you getting yourself into? Are you crazy?"

> Satan comes immediately and takes away the word that was sown in their hearts.
>
> Jesus, in Mark 4:15

These tactics of Satan go back to the Garden of Eden. He twisted God's words as he spoke to Eve, to make her doubtful of God: "Has God indeed said, 'You shall not eat of every tree of the garden'?" (Genesis 3:1).

He uses the same strategy against us. The enemy will say things like, "Is God's Word really true? Do you think God has *really* forgiven you?" It's simply a tactic he keeps using over and over with new believers.

But the enemy's temptations also seem to be targeted toward mature believers who happen to be making a difference in the kingdom of God. The devil has little need to spend a lot of time on many other believers because they're already where he wants them—immobilized. As C. H. Spurgeon said, "You don't kick a dead horse."

Are you only a "dead horse," or a truly worthwhile target
for the devil's attacks?

BECAUSE...

205

When you say, "Lord, use me. Let my life make a difference," then know this: The enemy will not be standing back to watch. Instead, he'll attack you. You'd better expect it, and brace yourself for it.

The Lord's promise to His people...

I am the vine, you are the branches. He who abides in Me, and I in him, bears much fruit; for without Me you can do nothing.
JESUS, IN JOHN 15:5

If you're never tempted or never come under spiritual attack, then you're either dead or worthless! On the other hand, if you're facing temptation and attack, that's a good indication you're on the right track.

With God in prayer...

Give thanks to God for His full help that's available to you in resisting temptation.

Because life is a spiritual battle...

How can you brace yourself *today* for approaching temptations?

Your own reflections... personal application... personal prayer points...

Wednesday

THE GOSPEL'S IMPACT

When the Lord Jesus spoke to Paul on the Damascus Road—after blinding Paul with a blast of light, He gave Paul one of the clearest descriptions in all of Scripture of how the gospel touches lives.

Late in the Book of Acts, as Paul stands as a prisoner before King Agrippa, he recalls these words from the Lord Jesus: "I am going to send you to the Gentiles, to open their eyes so they may turn from darkness to light, and from the power of Satan to God. Then they will receive forgiveness for their sins and be given a place among God's people, who are set apart by faith in me" (Acts 26:17–18 NLT).

Here, as Jesus describes what's involved when the gospel brings people to salvation, we see three steps:

One, your eyes are opened.

Two, you turn from darkness to light.

> I have come as a light into the world, that whoever believes in Me should not abide in darkness.
>
> Jesus, in John 12:46

Three, you turn from the power of Satan to God.

And as a result, you're forgiven and receive adoption and an inheritance in God's family.

> I have not come to call the righteous, but sinners, to repentance.
>
> Jesus, in Luke 5:32

Many people have taken step one, but they've never made it to step two. They've had their eyes opened, and they've seen that there's a God and there's a devil. They've seen that Jesus Christ is the answer to their problems and that they need to trust in Him and turn from their sin. They intellectually agree with these things, and they've recognized that there's a choice to be made. But they haven't taken steps two or three, which is *turning* from darkness to light and from the power of Satan to God.

And until they've taken those steps, they aren't truly converted.

The Lord's promise to His people...

I am the light of the world. He who follows Me shall not walk in darkness, but have the light of life.
JESUS, IN JOHN 8:12

With God in prayer...

Give thanks to the Lord for how His Spirit has opened your eyes and convicted you to turn from darkness to light.

Because Jesus came to call sinners to repentance...

Do you know of unbelievers whose eyes are opened to the gospel's truth, but who have not taken the step of actually turning from darkness to light? If so, pray for them now, asking God to move their hearts, by the Holy Spirit's conviction, to a true repentance.

Your own reflections... personal application... personal prayer points...

Thursday

KEEPING PACE

I heard about one man who always made New Year's resolutions. One year he decided, "I will not get annoyed when Sam and Charlie make jokes about my baldness."

The next year it was, "I won't get upset when Charlie and Sam kid me about my hairpiece."

In the following year: "I will not lose my temper when Sam and Charlie laugh at me for wearing a girdle."

Then the next year: "I will not speak anymore to Charlie and Sam."

That's our tendency, isn't it? We adjust our resolutions as time passes because we're unable to keep them. But we don't need a *resolution;* we need a *solution*—a spiritual solution, and it's found in the pages of Scripture.

Have you been seeking to rely on "resolutions"—instead of finding true solutions?

In Philippians 3, the apostle Paul helps us understand what our priorities should be. On more than one occasion, he used athletic metaphors to describe the Christian life. In this passage, he compares it to running a race: "I strain to reach the end of the race and receive the prize" (Philippians 3:14 NLT). But we need to understand this is not a fifty-yard dash. It's a long-distance run. That's why we must pace ourselves.

It isn't all that significant if you've held first place in a race for nine out of ten laps. What truly matters is the last lap. Whoever crosses the finish line first is the winner.

Let us run with **endurance** the race that
God has set before us.

Hebrews 12:1 NLT

The problem is that a lot of people have a yo-yo relationship with God—up and down. Either they're experiencing the ultimate spiritual high or they're down in the dumps. We need spiritual *consistency*. And we need God's help to stay with it. If we want to win in the race of life, we need to learn to pace ourselves.

> The Lord's promise to His people...
>
> He who endures to the end will be saved.
> JESUS, IN MATTHEW 10:22

With God in prayer...

Give thanks to your Lord and Savior for the race of life that He has planned for you in your life on earth.

Because we need to pace ourselves...

What steady progress can you make *today* in running the spiritual race that God has called you to? What specific things do you need to do right away?

Your own reflections... personal application... personal prayer points...

Friday

DROPPING EXCESS BAGGAGE

I'm the kind of person who likes to drag a lot of stuff with me when I travel. I've been traveling for many years, yet I still overpack. But excess baggage makes traveling more complicated.

In the same way, when you're running the race of life, you need to run light. Sometimes we drag along a lot of excess weight. But the Bible tells us to "strip off every weight that slows us down, especially the sin that so easily hinders our progress" (Hebrews 12:1 NLT). Sin is sin, and there are certain non-negotiables to which we must hold fast.

> I run in the path of your commands,
> for you have set my heart free.
> Psalm 119:32 NIV

But even apart from sin, there might be something that's a weight in your life that may not necessarily be a weight in another's life. There may be something you're doing that isn't necessarily sinful, but it's impeding your spiritual progress.

Periodically, I need to take stock of my life as a Christian and look at the things I'm doing with my time. I need to ask myself the question, "Is it a wing or a weight? Is it speeding me on my way spiritually, or is it slowing me down? Is it increasing my spiritual appetite, or is it dulling it?"

How often we get so busy doing a lot of things that seem significant at the time, but really aren't all that important. We need to ask ourselves if we really need to do all those things. Are they slowing you down? Lay aside the weight and the sin that hinders your progress.

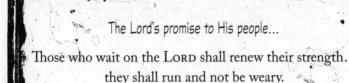

The Lord's promise to His people...

Those who wait on the LORD shall renew their strength...
they shall run and not be weary.

ISAIAH 40:31

With God in prayer...

For the spiritual race that lies before you, express your commitment and
your desire to know the joy of *running well*.

Because God has a race for you to run...

Take stock of how you're spending your time and energy. Is there
anything in your routine or schedule that's a significant drag on your
spiritual life? Something that's consistently dulling you spiritually? What
changes do you need to make? What weights do you need to drop?

Your own reflections... personal application... personal prayer points...

THROUGH THE FIRE

When I've gone through any kind of suffering in my life, it has always changed me in a way I cannot describe.

Hopefully trials will make us a little more compassionate, a little more sensitive, a little more caring toward others when *they* go through a hardship. It might be difficult to understand, but God is working toward a goal in our lives—to make us more like Christ.

There will be difficult things you go through that you won't understand and that you won't be able to easily explain. In reality, those things are inwardly forming you into the image of Jesus. You might not fully appreciate those things right now, or ever in this life. But through the suffering and through the valleys, you'll be made more and more into the likeness of Jesus Christ.

> So we don't look at the **troubles** we can see right now; rather, we look forward to what we have not yet seen. For the troubles we see will soon be over, but the **joys** to come will last **forever**.
>
> 2 Corinthians 4:18 NLT

The good news is that trials are temporary. According to 2 Corinthians 4:17, "Our present troubles are quite small and won't last very long. Yet they produce for us an immeasurably great glory that will last forever!" (NLT).

When God permits His children to go into the furnace, He always keeps an eye on the clock and a hand on the thermostat. If we rebel, He may have to reset the clock. But if we submit, He won't permit us to suffer one minute too long. He won't give us more than we can handle.

For You, O God, have tested us; You have refined
us as silver is refined.... We went through fire and
through water; but You brought us out to rich fulfillment.

Psalm 66:10-12

Maybe you're experiencing some form of difficulty right now. Maybe you're even going through a fiery trial. If so, know this: God is aware, and fully involved.

The Lord's promise to His people...

When you pass through the waters, I will be with you;
and through the rivers, they shall not overflow you.
When you walk through the fire, you shall not be burned,
nor shall the flame scorch you. For I am the LORD your God.

ISAIAH 43:2–3

With God in prayer...

Give thanks to the Lord for how temporary our trials and hardships really are, in light of eternity.

Because trials make us more like Christ...

In your typical response to trials, what rebellious tendencies need to be replaced by submission?

Your own reflections... personal application... personal prayer points...

RELATIONSHIP OBSTACLES

The Bible tells the story of the great patriarch, Abraham, who was called by the Lord to leave his homeland and his family. God would lead him to a land where he'd never been. Abraham wanted to take everyone along, but the problem was that many of his family members were unbelievers. They were dragging Abraham down spiritually.

Most notable among them was his nephew, Lot. God told Abraham to part company with Lot, but it took him awhile to obey. As long as Lot was hanging around, God's blessing was not upon Abraham in the way it could have been.

Finally, Abraham obeyed the Lord, and he and Lot parted ways. Then God's blessing came upon Abraham once again.

As you're running your race as a Christian, you may find yourself being hindered by someone. Is there someone in your life who's slowing you down, as Lot did with Abraham? After spending time with certain people, do you feel spiritually drained?

You were running a good race.
Who cut in on you and kept you from obeying the truth?
Galatians 5:7 NIV

Perhaps you've thought, *That person brought out the worst in me. They didn't help me in any way.* While we want to minister to people and reach them with the gospel, we must be careful not to do so at the expense of our own spiritual lives. There might be someone who's slowing you down in the race of life.

Is any person hindering you from doing what
God has called you to do?

BECAUSE...

215

Is someone dragging you down spiritually? You need to ask yourself, "Is this person a wing or a weight? Is he or she speeding me on my way or slowing me down?" Running the race isn't just running toward what's right. It's also running away from what's wrong.

> The Lord's promise to His people...
>
> It is good for me to draw near to God.
> PSALM 73:28

With God in prayer...

Take time to thank God for friendships and relationships in your life that truly build you up spiritually.

Because God has a race for you to run...

Evaluate your relationships to consider whether some of them are hindering you spiritually. Do you need to cut back on your involvement with someone, to free you up spiritually? Is there a relationship you need to terminate altogether? Ask the Lord for wisdom about this, because the most important thing is winning the race of life. "Run from anything that stimulates youthful lust. Follow anything that makes you want to do right. Pursue faith and love and peace, and enjoy the companionship of those who call on the Lord with pure hearts" (2 Timothy 2:22 NLT).

Your own reflections... personal application... personal prayer points...

Tuesday

THE RIGHT MOTIVE FOR RUNNING

Back when I was in high school, I ran track and field. Whenever I knew a pretty girl was watching, I always ran faster. I wanted to impress her.

If you're a Christian because someone else is or because you want to impress someone, I have news for you: You aren't going to make it in the race of life. You must run this race for the Lord Himself. That's what will give you the strength to keep going.

> Everything else is worthless when compared with the priceless gain of knowing Christ Jesus my Lord. I have discarded everything else, counting it all as garbage, so that I may have Christ.
>
> Philippians 3:8 NLT

For the apostle Paul, the motivating goal for running his own race was all about *knowing* Jesus Christ: "That I may know Him and the power of His resurrection, and the fellowship of His sufferings" (Philippians 3:10). Notice that Paul didn't say, "That I may know *about* Him." We know about a lot of things today. We know about certain celebrities. You may have read articles that describe these people. You may know a lot about them. But you really don't know them.

> By this we know that we know Him, if we keep His commandments.
>
> 1 John 2:3

In the same way, you can say, "I know all about Jesus. I know all about the Bible." But Paul didn't say he wanted to know *about* Jesus. He said he wanted to *know* Him. And there's a difference. Truly knowing Him comes only through a growing relationship with Jesus Christ.

The Bible teaches us that as we "run with endurance the race that is set before us," we need to be *"looking unto Jesus,* the author and finisher of our faith" (Hebrews 12:1–2). That's the right motive for running. That's what will help you finish the race with flying colors.

The Lord's promise to His people...

I write to you, little children, because you have known the Father.
1 JOHN 2:13

With God in prayer...

With true gratefulness, review the joy and peace and fulfillment you have experienced in your heart through getting better acquainted with Jesus Christ.

Because of the joy of knowing Jesus Christ...

Evaluate your own desire and commitment to know Christ better. Is it as strong now as ever? Is it growing stronger?

Your own reflections... personal application... personal prayer points...

DON'T LOOK BACK

If you've ever have run a race and looked over your shoulder to see what your competitor was doing, you know that looking back can break your stride and ultimately cause you to lose the race.

Likewise, if you want to run the race of life successfully, don't look back.

> But one thing I do, forgetting those things which are behind and reaching forward to those things which are ahead, I press toward the goal.
>
> Philippians 3:13-14

Along these lines, Paul teaches us the value of "forgetting those things which are behind" and instead "reaching forward to those things which are ahead" (Philippians 3:13). If you're going to walk with the Lord, you must forget the things that are behind. This word *forget* doesn't mean failing to remember as much as it means no longer being influenced or affected by the past.

Here's what you need to do as you move forward in your Christian life: Let go of the past. While you may not be able to erase the past from your memory, you don't need to let those things influence you.

Sometimes we dredge up the things God has forgiven and forgotten. The Lord says, "I will remember their sins no more" (Jeremiah 31:34 NIV), yet many times we'll bring up past sins in our mind, forgetting the fact that our God has a big eraser. Why should we choose to remember what God has chosen to forget? If God has forgiven my sins and forgotten them, I need to leave them behind, learn from my mistakes, not do the same thing again, and move forward.

Do not remember the former things, nor consider the things of old.

Behold, I will do a new thing, now it shall spring forth.

Isaiah 43:18-19

In addition to forgetting our sins, there's a sense in which we should also forget our victories. Certainly, we're to thank God for them. But past victory doesn't guarantee victory today.

Remember each day is a *new* day with *new* opportunities.

The Lord's promise to His people...

Behold, I make all things new.

REVELATION 21:5

With God in prayer...

Give thanks to God that the blood of Jesus Christ covers over the sins of your past.

Because God has a race for you to run...

Are there things in the past that still occupy too much of your mind and heart? Any resentment, regrets, frustrations, or failures that loom too large in your thoughts and feelings? Let go of them today.

Your own reflections... personal application... personal prayer points...

FORWARD TO THE GOAL

In the race of life, Paul experienced the power of "forgetting those things which are behind and reaching forward to those things which are ahead"; therefore he could say, "I press toward the goal" (Philippians 3:13–14).

This word *press* implies strong exertion. The picture is of a runner whose every muscle is burning. He can see the finish line. He envisions the medal. He hasn't far to go in this race, and he must press on.

It's the same in our lives as Christians. There are times when it just gets hard. But that's when we learn what it means to walk by faith and not by feeling. You can't live on an emotional high as a Christian; you must pace yourself in this race you're running. You can't expect to have some great emotional encounter with God every time you go to church. Sometimes you will; sometimes you won't. Growing up and learning to walk by faith—to keep *pressing on* by faith—is part of spiritual maturity. It means being "like a great athlete eager to run the race" (Psalm 19:5 NLT).

When you first made a commitment to Christ, you discovered the joy and wonderful peace that comes from being forgiven. But never forget this is a journey by faith. You must keep pushing forward even when it gets hard.

Maybe you've found yourself in a place where you're dragging burdens, sins, or other things along. Maybe you find you're not even sure why you're running the race anymore. Maybe you've become discouraged.

If so, look up and remember that you're running for Jesus. Your goal is fully knowing Him, and being fully in His presence.

Prepare your **minds** for action; be self-controlled; set your hope fully on the grace to be given you when Jesus Christ is **revealed**.

1 Peter 1:13 NIV

Two thousand years ago, He loved you so much that He went to the cross and died there. He shed His blood for you. Then He rose again from the dead.

Because He did that for you, you can live for Him today. He'll give you the strength you need.

> The Lord's promise to His people...
>
> The God of all grace...will himself restore, confirm, strengthen, and establish you.
>
> 1 PETER 5:10 ESV

With God in prayer...

Ask the Lord Jesus Christ for the strength you need *today* to keep running well in the race of life He has laid out before you. And acknowledge before Him that He Himself is your goal.

Because God has a race for you to run...

Evaluate clearly and honestly the most significant hardships and obstacles you are currently facing in the race of life. How can you apply Christ's help in overcoming these?

Your own reflections... personal application... personal prayer points...

Friday

PLAYING BY THE RULES

We all know that if you participate in an athletic event, you must play by the established rules. You can't make up your own.

If anyone competes in athletics, he is not **crowned** unless he competes according to the **rules.**
2 Timothy 2:5

You can't go the baseball field and say, "Here's how it works: If I hit the ball eight feet, that's a home run." That isn't the way the game is played. And even if you hit the ball out of the park, you still must cross and touch every single base. If you miss one base, that home run doesn't count, and you're disqualified.

If you want to compete in events like the Olympics or the Tour de France, one of the rules is that athletes are prohibited from using drugs like steroids to enhance their performance. Sometimes the winner of an event will even be stripped of their victory when a drug test reveals the use of some prohibited substance.

Remember that in a race everyone runs, but only **one** person gets the prize. You also must run in such a way that you will **win.**
1 Corinthians 9:24 NLT

In the same way, this race of life we're running has a rulebook. It's called the Bible. It's not for us to pick and choose what parts of the Bible we like. You can't say, "I accept certain truths in the Bible. I like the part about God's love and forgiveness. But this part about denying yourself and taking up the cross—I reject that!"

You can't do that. If you're going to run this race, and run to win, you must play by the rules God has given to you in Scripture. We must play by the rules, or we'll be disqualified.

The Lord's promise to His people...

Be faithful until death, and I will give you the crown of life.
JESUS, IN REVELATION 2:10

With God in prayer...

Ask God to clearly show you the rules you need to follow most closely at this time in your life.

Because you win if you follow the rules...

What "rules" from God are you most likely to bend or break?

Your own reflections... personal application... personal prayer points...

PRAYER FROM THE RIGHT PERSON

In the Book of James we read this: "The prayer of a righteous person has great power as it is working" (James 5:16 ESV).

When you come to those words "a righteous person," maybe you think, *That counts me out. I certainly wouldn't consider myself righteous.* But if you've put your faith in Jesus Christ, then I would beg to differ.

God has made Christ Himself to actually be *our* righteousness: "He is the source of your life in Christ Jesus, whom God made our wisdom and our righteousness" (1 Corinthians 1:30 ESV). Because of what Christ has accomplished for you, and your trust in Him as Savior and Lord, you are righteous in your position or standing before God—and so am I.

> He shall bring forth your **righteousness** as the light.
>
> Psalm 37:6

When you first put your faith in Christ, part of the work of justification taking place in that moment is that not only are you forgiven of every wrong you've ever done, but the righteousness of Christ is also imputed into your account.

Imagine that you were penniless and $20 million in debt. Then one day, someone came along, paid your debt, and deposited $100 million into your account. That's the idea of our righteousness in Christ.

So positionally before God, you're a righteous person.

> The earnest prayer of a righteous person has great power and wonderful results. Elijah was as human as we are, and yet when he prayed **earnestly** that no rain would fall, **none** fell for the next three and a half years!
>
> James 5:16-17 NLT

BECAUSE...

James cites Elijah as an example of a righteous man. Most people think of Elijah as a super prophet, yet Elijah was a very human guy. He had his lapses. But he prayed, and God answered his prayer.

So in spite of our flaws, we can know our prayers still can be powerful and effective. 225

The Lord's promise to His people...

God alone made it possible for you to be in Christ Jesus.
For our benefit God made Christ to be wisdom itself.
He is the one who made us acceptable to God. He made us
pure and holy, and he gave himself to purchase our freedom.

1 CORINTHIANS 1:30 NLT

With God in prayer...

Fully express your thanksgiving for the fact that Jesus Christ is *your* righteousness.

Because Jesus Christ is our righteousness...

On the basis of your righteousness in Christ, who do you need to pray for now, as a righteous person praying with great power (James 5:16)?

Your own reflections... personal application... personal prayer points...

BE RECONCILED

The Bible teaches us to confess our sins to other believers—"Confess your sins to each other" (James 5:16 NLT). This doesn't mean we must confess our sins to a pastor or to a priest in order to be absolved. Rather, we should *first* confess our sins to God and then to each other.

This passage also doesn't mean that every time you've sinned, you need to come to church, stand up at some point in the service, and say, "Excuse me. I have an announcement to make. I went over the speed limit today. That was a sin." You don't need to publicly state every sin you've committed.

But if you've specifically sinned against someone, then you ought to go specifically to that person and repent of it. If there has been a specific wrong done, you should try to rectify it.

> I appeal to you, brothers, by the name of our Lord Jesus Christ,
> that all of you agree and that there be no divisions among you,
> but that you be united in the same mind and the same judgment.
>
> 1 Corinthians 1:10 ESV

If there's unresolved conflict between you and another believer, it can hinder your prayer life. That's why Jesus said, "If you are standing before the altar in the Temple, offering a sacrifice to God, and you suddenly remember that someone has something against you, leave your sacrifice there beside the altar. Go and be reconciled to that person. Then come and offer your sacrifice to God" (Matthew 5:23–24 NLT). You might want to pray, "Lord, is there anyone I've sinned against, anyone I've hurt, anyone I've wronged? If so, show me who that person is."

Be humble and gentle. Be patient with each other, making allowance
for each other's faults because of your love. Always keep yourselves
united in the Holy Spirit, and bind yourselves together with peace.

Ephesians 4:2-3 NLT

If God brings a broken relationship to your attention, deal with
it. For instance, let's say you passed along information about another
person, then later realized this information was false. You certainly owe
that person an apology! And what about all the others you passed along
that gossip to? You need to let them know the truth as well. Let your
repentance be as widely known as your sin.

> The Lord's promise to His people...
>
> In Christ Jesus you who once were far off
> have been brought near by the blood of Christ.
>
> EPHESIANS 2:13

With God in prayer...

Make this your request: "Lord, is there anyone I've sinned against? Is
there anyone I've hurt? Is there anyone I've wronged? Have I gossiped
about someone? If I have, show me, so I can make things right with that
person."

Because God brings reconciliation...

In your life, what relational issues need your careful attention today?
Remember: Until there is reconciliation, a break in any relationship can
hinder your ability to approach the throne of God.

Your own reflections... personal application... personal prayer points...

Tuesday

GOD'S PROMISE TO THE PERSECUTED

The church of Smyrna was a group of believers who braved persecution and other afflictions, and Jesus' words to them are for all suffering believers:

> I know about your suffering and your poverty—but you are rich! I know the slander of those opposing you.... Don't be afraid of what you are about to suffer.... Remain faithful even when facing death, and I will give you the crown of life. (Revelation 2:9–10 NLT)

Of course, we think suffering and persecution are the worst things possible. We don't want to face them. We don't want hardship. We don't want harassment. We don't want persecution of any kind in our lives. In fact, we try to avoid it at all costs.

What is your **deepest**, most consistent attitude toward persecution and **hardship**?

But there's a special blessing promised to the persecuted believer. Jesus said,

> God blesses you when you are mocked and persecuted and lied about because you are my followers. Be happy about it! Be very glad! For a great reward awaits you in heaven. And remember, the ancient prophets were persecuted, too. (Matthew 5:11–12 NLT)

Jesus also said that we, as His followers, should expect persecution: "When the world hates you, remember it hated me before it hated you. The world would love you if you belonged to it, but you don't. I chose you to come out of the world, and so it hates you. Do you remember what I told you? 'A servant is not greater than the master.' Since they persecuted me, naturally they will persecute you. And if they had listened to me, they would listen to you!" (John 15:18–20 NLT).

God may allow persecution into your life. He may allow hardship. He may allow difficulty. He may allow a thorn in the flesh to keep you dependent upon Him. And whether you like it or not, it's for your own good spiritually.

> The Lord's promise to His people...
>
> Remember the word that I said to you, "A servant is not greater than his master." If they persecuted Me, they will also persecute you.
>
> JESUS, IN JOHN 15:20

With God in prayer...

Give thanks to the Lord Jesus for how He endured the world's hatred and persecution.

Because He has promised persecution...

How ready are you for facing greater persecution than you have previously known? Should you be more prepared? If so, what should you do?

Your own reflections... personal application... personal prayer points...

Wednesday

THE PERSECUTED CHURCH

The message of Jesus to the church of Smyrna, which represents the persecuted church, is the briefest of the seven messages Christ gave to seven different churches in the Book of Revelation.

By the way, the name *Smyrna* is related to the word *myrrh*, which is an aromatic ingredient used in perfumes and incense. The city of Smyrna developed, processed, and exported myrrh.

In the Bible, myrrh is essentially an embalming element. The wise men who came to visit Jesus as a child brought gifts of gold, frankincense, and myrrh. When Jesus hung on the cross, He was offered vinegar with myrrh to help deaden the pain, but He refused it.

As myrrh is crushed, it gives off a beautiful scent. Like the myrrh from which its name was derived, the church of Smyrna was a church that was crushed.

Jesus told this particular church that they were going to undergo severe trials. And in those days, and throughout the early centuries of the Christian church's existence, there were great persecutions against the church in which vast numbers of Christians lost their lives. But instead of destroying the church, persecution actually strengthened it, as the believers obeyed the Lord's word: "Do not fear any of those things which you are about to suffer.... Be faithful until death, and I will give you the crown of life" (Revelation 2:10).

I have fought a good fight, I have finished the race, and I have remained faithful. And now the prize awaits me—the crown of righteousness that the Lord, the righteous Judge, will give me on that great day of his return. And the prize is not just for me but for all who eagerly look forward to his glorious return.

2 Timothy 4:7-8 NLT

BECAUSE . . . .

Persecution has a way of separating real believers from false ones. If you knew you would lose your life for professing Christ as your Savior and Lord, would you speak up for Him? Or would you hide your faith?

The Lord's promise to His people...

Then everyone will stand in awe, proclaiming the mighty acts of God, realizing all the amazing things he does.

PSALM 64:9 NLT

With God in prayer...

It's been said that Christians are a lot like teabags: You don't know what they're made of until you put them in hot water. It's often in the "hot waters" of persecution that we as believers discover what we're really made of. As you contemplate the likelihood of future sufferings and persecution, what fears enter your heart? Bring these before the Lord, and allow Him to deal with them.

Because severe trials will come...

If the Lord has a time of "crushing" in store for you soon, how can you prepare for it?

Your own reflections... personal application... personal prayer points...

Thursday

SILENCE FROM HEAVEN

In His message to the church of Smyrna in the Book of Revelation, it's interesting to observe that Jesus had nothing in the way of correction to say to them. He corrected the other six churches in various ways, but He didn't correct this one. Why?

Because there was nothing to correct. These believers were living godly lives. They were laying them down for the Lord.

It's also worth noting that He didn't offer a single word of commendation. Obviously, these believers were extremely pleasing to the Lord, because a special crown awaited those who suffered like this. But instead of a pat on the back, there was a warning that it would get worse: "Do not fear any of those things which you are about to suffer" (Revelation 2:10).

> You will be hated by all for My name's sake.
> Jesus, in Matthew 10:22

It would have been nice if Jesus had said, "It's tough now, but everything will get better. Just hang in there." But instead He was saying, "It's going to get worse." Instead of promising them better times here on earth, He focused their attention on eternal rewards. He was saying, "If you're faithful, there'll be a crown waiting for you."

When we're going through an extreme trial, a time of testing or persecution, we may long for a special word from the Lord. But here's something to think about: It may be that the Lord's silence is His highest commendation. It may be that silence is a sign not of disapproval, but of approval.

232

BECAUSE . . . .

A case in point is the church of Smyrna. There wasn't a word of commendation for them from the Lord, but it's obvious He was pleased with them.

If you're going through a time of suffering or hardship, perhaps Jesus is saying, "I know what you're going through." And maybe that silence from heaven is not so silent after all.

> The Lord's promise to His people...
>
> I will look to the LORD; I will wait for the God
> of my salvation; my God will hear me.
> MICAH 7:7

With God in prayer...

Thank the Lord for speaking to you faithfully and often through the pages of the Bible.

Because He knows all that you're going through...

If there will soon be a time of "silence" from the Lord in your life, how will you respond to this?

Your own reflections... personal application... personal prayer points...

Friday

PLAYING AROUND WITH SIN

People will sometimes walk into a place of temptation and think, "This is no problem. I can handle it. I'm strong."

Famous last words.

Those were Samson's thoughts. He knew he was strong. The Philistines had repeatedly tried to kill him, yet he came out ahead every time. On one occasion, he killed one thousand Philistines with a bone he picked up off the ground. No one could stop him.

In what areas, if any, are you **tempted** *to think of yourself as not being vulnerable to* **sin?**

So the devil changed his tactics. He couldn't bring Samson down on the battlefield, so he decided to bring him down in the bedroom. He sent a beautiful young girl named Delilah into Samson's life.

Delilah was up-front about her intentions. She said, "Please tell me what makes you so strong and what it would take to tie you up securely" (Judges 16:6 NLT). That should have been a major sign to Samson that this wasn't a good relationship. But he didn't take her seriously. He teased her with various answers, getting closer and closer to revealing the truth, until one day, he told Delilah everything. He had been under a certain vow since his birth, and an angel from the Lord had commanded that his hair never be cut. That was the key to Samson's strength.

Delilah lulled Samson to sleep with his head in her lap, and she called in a man to shave off his hair, making his capture certain. And his **strength** *left him.*

Judges 16:19 NLT

The next time Samson fell asleep, Delilah gave him a buzz cut. Then he found out what happens when you play around with sin: Sin plays around with you. As a result, Samson's life came to a premature and tragic end.

We need to have a healthy respect for the power of temptation and for the effectiveness of Satan's strategies against us.

> The Lord's promise to His people...
>
> For the backsliding of the simple shall slay them,
> and the careless ease of [self-confident] fools shall destroy them.
> PROVERBS 1:32 AMP

With God in prayer...

Thank the Lord for the abundant teaching He gives us in Scripture about how to overcome temptation.

Because Satan's strategies are powerfully effective...

Are you playing around with any sin right now? If so, confess this, look to God for strength, and move on.

Your own reflections... personal application... personal prayer points...

Weekend

REAL CHANGE

Sometimes we hear about commitments to Christ being made by movie stars, musical entertainers, sports figures—and politicians, whose "conversions" usually take place around election time, of course. (After the elections, we seldom hear about their great faith in God.) Thankfully there *are* celebrities and elected officials who are genuine believers; but many who profess faith never seem to show any evidence of it.

Then there are people who say they're believers, but a month or two later, they go back to their old ways again. They say, "I tried Christianity, but it didn't work for me." Others will turn to God only when they hit hard times. A while later, you see them going back to their old ways, and you wonder what happened. I would suggest that many of these people never were converted at all. In reality, they never really found Christ. They went through the motions, but Jesus Christ never became a part of their lives. Often, they end up worse than before.

When people escape from the wicked ways of the world by learning about our Lord and Savior Jesus Christ and then get tangled up with sin and become its slave again, they are worse off than before.

2 Peter 2:20 NLT

When Christ truly comes into our lives, He takes up residence. And He doesn't do just a basic housecleaning; He does a *thorough* one. There's real change. But when a house has only been lightly swept—when someone has made only outward changes—he or she is still vulnerable to the enemy. That's why every human being must recognize the futility of simply turning over a new leaf or making a few New Year's resolutions. The problem is deeper than our outward moral behavior. We must have Christ take up residence in our lives and change us from the inside out.

BECAUSE . . .

236

The Lord's promise to His people...

Those who become Christians become new persons.
They are not the same anymore, for the old life is gone.
A new life has begun!

2 CORINTHIANS 5:17 NLT

With God in prayer...

Give your thanks to God for the true change He has accomplished in your life since you became a Christian.

Because Christ changes us from the inside out...

What new changes do you sense that Christ wants to accomplish now in your life?

Your own reflections... personal application... personal prayer points...

Monday

HOPING FOR JUDGMENT

In the book of Jonah, when God first told this man, "Get up and go," we might wonder why Jonah didn't quickly obey.

> The LORD gave this message to Jonah...: "Get up and go to the great city of Nineveh! Announce my judgment against it because I have seen how wicked its people are."
>
> Jonah 1:1-2 NLT

We have to realize that Jonah was a patriotic Israelite who loved his people. Nineveh, however, was the capital of Assyria, the enemy of Israel. So when God told Jonah to go there and preach, Jonah probably thought at first, *I'm kind of happy to know He's planning to judge them. It's one less enemy we'll have to contend with.* But Jonah knew that God had this tendency to forgive. So his fear was that God would let the Assyrians off the hook.

Jonah didn't care about the Ninevites. His procrastination and personal prejudice was stronger than any passion for the lost. So God's judgment against Nineveh suited Jonah just fine. In his mind, they certainly deserved it. In fact, he probably hoped God would carry out His judgment quickly.

Sometimes we can be that way. We may take perverse pleasure in knowing that certain people who really irritate us or harass us will someday be going to hell. But certainly that's not the attitude we should have as believers.

The fact is that we *all* deserve to go to hell. We *all* deserve judgment from God.

Jesus didn't say, "Hate your enemies, and hope that their judgment

238

BECAUSE . . .

comes soon." Rather, He said, "Love your enemies! Pray for those who persecute you!" (Matthew 5:44 NLT).

Remember, you once were on your way to hell. So was I—and I try never to forget it.

> The Lord's promise to His people…
>
> Whoever calls on the name of the LORD shall be saved.
>
> JOEL 2:32

With God in prayer…

Is there anyone whose condemnation from God you've secretly hoped ·for? If so, repent of this sin, and pray for that person's salvation in Christ.

Because God wants all to be saved…

Make a renewed effort to speak with nonbelievers whose salvation you may not have been concerned about. Ask God to lead you to the right person.

Your own reflections… personal application… personal prayer points…

Tuesday

RUNNING THE WRONG WAY

Even with the passing of thousands of years, it's interesting to see how the frail and foolish tendencies of human beings remain the same.

When we don't want to do something that's the will of God, we try to run from Him—just like Jonah did. When God told Jonah to go and preach to the city of Nineveh, Jonah *went* all right—the opposite way. He was trying to escape from God as well as from his own conscience.

> But Jonah got up and went in the **opposite** direction in order to get away from the LORD....
>
> Jonah 1:3 NLT

It's easy for us to criticize Jonah in this situation, but in reality, don't we as Christians sometimes turn away from our own marching orders given from the Lord Himself? He has commanded us, "Go and make disciples of all the nations, baptizing them in the name of the Father and the Son and the Holy Spirit" (Matthew 28:19 NLT). Have we done that?

In many ways, some of us may be just like Jonah.

The real message in the book of Jonah is that of God's longsuffering, patience, and willingness to forgive those who are willing to stop running from Him and instead run *to* Him.

> God...commands all people everywhere to **repent**.
>
> Acts 17:30 ESV

There is JOY in the presence of the angels of
God over one sinner who repents.

Jesus, in Luke 15:10

Maybe, like Jonah, you've been trying to run away from God. Maybe
you know the will of God for your life, but you've said, "I know what God
wants me to do. I know I shouldn't be doing what I'm doing, but I want
to do it anyway. It's what I choose to do."

Even if you've turned your back on God, God hasn't turned His back
on you. No matter what you've done, God stands ready to forgive. But
you must return to Him.

The Lord's promise to His people...

People who cover over their sins will not prosper.
But if they confess and forsake them, they will receive mercy.

PROVERBS 28:13 NLT

With God in prayer...

Is there a need for repentance in your life? Do not delay it a moment
longer. Come to God—and turn away from your sin.

Because God is ready to forgive...

Who do you know that should hear *today* the message of God's
forgiveness in Christ Jesus? Make your plans to meet and speak with this
person.

Your own reflections... personal application... personal prayer points...

Wednesday

GOD GETS THE LAST WORD

Jonah was the Lord's servant—but he behaved as a wayward child running from the Lord. And the Bible says that when it comes to dealing with His own, "The Lord disciplines those he loves" (Hebrews 12:6 NLT). Because of His love for us as our Father, God will get our attention when we're going the wrong way, just as He did with Jonah.

> Know then in your **heart** that, as a man disciplines his son, the LORD your God disciplines you.
>
> Deuteronomy 8:5 ESV

I think we all know what this is like. When we're about to do something we know we shouldn't do, there'll be that internal red flag, that sense of conviction from the Holy Spirit which insists, *"Don't do this! This is the wrong direction!"* Sometimes God will even put blockades in our path in the form of other believers. Maybe you're about to do something you know you shouldn't, when suddenly you run into a Christian friend. You think, *Lord, you're making this hard.* Yes, He is—because He loves you. As your Father, He doesn't want you going in the wrong direction.

In Psalm 119:67 we read this personal confession: "Before I was afflicted I went astray, but now I keep Your word." In other words, before the psalmist tasted the sting of discipline, he was doing what he wanted to do, but then the Lord got his attention through affliction.

As Jonah ran away from God's will, he boarded a ship headed across the sea. "But the LORD sent out a great wind on the sea, and there was a mighty tempest" (Jonah 1:4). That storm was the beginning of some serious discipline God brought into Jonah's life—just as He'll bring serious discipline into our lives when we're trying to escape His will.

I once heard Bible teacher Alan Redpath say that a man outside

God's will is a menace to himself and everyone else. It was true in Jonah's case, and for anyone who deliberately steps outside His will for our lives.

> The Lord's promise to His people...
>
> If they do not obey my decrees and fail to keep my commands,
> then I will punish their sin with the rod,
> and their disobedience with beating.
> PSALM 89:31–32 NLT

With God in prayer...

Offer sincere thanksgiving to your Father in heaven for His wise love for you—because He faithfully brings discipline into your life when you need it.

Because He lovingly disciplines you...

Are there any current hardships you're experiencing in life which may be God's way of disciplining you? Are you out of God's will—and if so, is it affecting other people around you? Recognize this for what it really is, and make the corrections *today* that you need to make.

Your own reflections... personal application... personal prayer points...

FLEE TEMPTATION

Luke's Gospel tells us how at one point during the Last Supper, Jesus turned to Simon Peter and said, "Simon, Simon! Indeed, Satan has asked for you, that he may sift you as wheat" (Luke 22:31).

I would be really concerned if Jesus said that to me. Here was Peter, spending time with the Lord and the other disciples. Everything was great. Then Jesus turned to the fisherman with these alarming words: "The devil has been asking for you."

"By name?"

"Yes—he wants you taken out of God's care and protection."

This wasn't sounding good at all. When the Lord spoke these words to Peter, I wonder if He paused for effect and looked at Peter before He went on to say this: "But I have prayed for you, that your faith should not fail; and when you have returned to Me, strengthen your brethren" (Luke 22:32).

Now that was good news! Jesus had been praying for Peter.

> Christ Jesus...is the one who died for us
> and was raised to life for us and is sitting
> at the place of highest honor next to God, pleading for us.
>
> Romans 8:34 NLT

We need to stand in God's strength and realize our vulnerability. We play a part in our own temptation, because Satan needs our cooperation to draw us in. For him to succeed, we must first listen to what he has to offer. Then we have to yield to it, and we have to desire what he's presenting to us. When there's no desire on our part, there's no temptation of any effect on his part.

Do you not know that to whom you present yourselves **slaves** to obey, you are that one's slaves whom you obey, whether of sin leading to death, or of **obedience** leading to righteousness?

Romans 6:16

So we want to keep our distance. Flee temptation, and don't leave a forwarding address.

The Lord's promise to His people...

He [Christ] is also able to save to the uttermost
those who come to God through Him, since
He always lives to make intercession for them.

HEBREWS 7:25

With God in prayer...

Give thanks to the Lord Jesus Christ for His interceding prayers for us.

Because Jesus Christ prays for you...

Based on your past, where is your faith most likely to fail? How can you depend more freely on Christ in this area?

Your own reflections... personal application... personal prayer points...

ONLY TWO CHOICES

As we look over the pages of history, it's interesting to read the statements that have been made about Christ.

Pontius Pilate said, "I find no fault in Him." Napoleon said, "I know men, and Jesus was no mere man." Strauss, the German rationalist, said, "Jesus was the highest model of religion." The French atheist Renan said, "He was the greatest among the sons of men." Theodore Parker said, "Jesus Christ was a youth with God in His heart." Robert Owen said, "He is the irreproachable one."

> Simon Peter answered, "You are the Messiah, the Son of the living God."
> Matthew 16:16 NLT

Yet all these titles and descriptions fall short of identifying Jesus for who He really was—the Son of God, God in human form, the Messiah.

> We have come to believe and know that You are the Christ, the Son of the living God.
> John 6:69

Many today would describe Jesus as a great moral teacher. But in his book *Mere Christianity*, C. S. Lewis responds to such a statement by saying that if this were the case, then Jesus was either a lunatic or a devil. He goes on to say, "Let us not come with any patronizing nonsense about His being a great human teacher. He has not left that open to us. He did not intend to."

BECAUSE . . .

We don't have the option of saying Jesus was a great moral teacher. How could He merely be a teacher and say the things He said with His exclusive claims of divinity? And what about saying He was the only way to God the Father? If it weren't true, then saying such a thing would certainly be worthy of blame.

So, Jesus really leaves us only two choices—either to accept Him, believing He is indeed God the Son, or to reject Him. But to say He was a great man or a mere moral teacher is simply not an option.

The Lord's promise to His people...

Blessed are those who have not seen and yet have believed.

JESUS, IN JOHN 20:29

With God in prayer...

Thank your Father in heaven for the grace and mercy He has shown to you in helping you choose to accept and believe in His Son, Jesus Christ.

Because Jesus is the Son of God, the Messiah...

Who should you be discussing the claims of Christ with?

Your own reflections... personal application... personal prayer points...

THE HARDEST TO REACH

At one point in the ministry of Jesus, we read that "even His brothers did not believe in Him" (John 7:5), and this remained true for them until after His resurrection. The Gospels also tell us of a time when his relatives came to take Him home, thinking He'd taken leave of His senses (Mark 3:21). This just goes to show that even if we as believers were to live perfect and flawless lives, it wouldn't necessarily convince someone of the truth of the gospel.

> He returned to Nazareth, his hometown. When he taught there in the synagogue, everyone was astonished.... And they were deeply offended and refused to believe in him. Then Jesus told them, "A prophet is honored everywhere except in his own hometown and among his own family."
>
> Matthew 13:54-57 NLT

We'll hear people say, "The reason I'm not a Christian is because there are so many hypocrites in the church." How do we answer that objection? Do we say it isn't true? Of course there are hypocrites in the church. We've all been hypocritical at one time or another. When it comes to living out the Christian witness we ought to live, all of us will fall short at times.

Jesus, on the other hand, lived a flawless, perfect life. He never sinned in any capacity. He never lied or stole or lost His temper. He never even sinned inwardly. Yet even with all that, some of those who were closest to Him still did not believe in Him—at least not right away. It took His resurrection from the dead to finally bring them around.

This should serve as a reminder that the hardest people to reach are often those unbelievers who are the closest to us, especially in our own families. A non-Christian home can often be an extremely difficult and hostile environment for a new believer.

> The Lord's promise to His people...
>
> "Is not My word like a fire?" says the LORD,
> "and like a hammer that breaks the rock in pieces?"
> JEREMIAH 23:29

With God in prayer...

Think of those unbelievers you know personally who seem hardest to reach with the gospel. Pray for their salvation.

Because God is the God of the impossible...

Pray *more* for those you know personally who seem hardest to reach with the gospel.

Your own reflections... personal application... personal prayer points...

CONTEMPLATING THE CROSS

I heard about a man who was trying to start his own religion, but it wasn't going well. He decided to approach the French statesman, Charles-Maurice de Talleyrand, and ask him what he should do to gain converts. The statesman told him, "I recommend you get yourself crucified, die, and then rise again on the third day."

Jesus' death on the cross and His resurrection on the third day is the cornerstone of the Christian faith. It's what sets our faith as Christians apart from the faith of all others.

> How we thank God, who gives us victory
> over sin and death through Jesus Christ our Lord!
> 1 Corinthians 15:57 NLT

Yet many view Christ's crucifixion as a rude interruption of what was an otherwise successful ministry. But the cross was at the forefront of the mind of Jesus Christ from the very beginning. He knew He was headed for the cross, and He spoke of it often.

The Bible calls Jesus "the Lamb slain from the foundation of the world" (Revelation 13:8)—letting us know that even before He came to this earth, a decision was made that He would ultimately go to the cross.

It was at the cross that God's righteous demands upon us were satisfied. It was at the cross that God and humanity were reconciled once again. It was at the cross that a decisive blow was dealt against Satan and his minions. It was at the cross that our very salvation was purchased. Therefore, we can never talk about the cross too much or contemplate it too often.

The Lord's promise to His people...

God demonstrates His own love toward us,
in that while we were still sinners, Christ died for us.
ROMANS 5:8

With God in prayer...

Thank God for the forgiveness of *your* sins, and for how it was purchased
through the death of His beloved Son Jesus.

Because Christ died for your sins...

Memorize a Scripture passage that speaks of what Christ did for us
through His death—such as Isaiah 53:6, Mark 10:45, Romans 3:23–24,
or 2 Corinthians 5:21.

Your own reflections... personal application... personal prayer points...

HE KNOWS

In the Book of Revelation, we find a message from the Lord Jesus Christ to the church at Ephesus.

In this particular church, the apostle Paul—and possibly the apostle John as well—had once been pastors. So the Ephesian believers had known excellent leadership in their history. But at the time the Book of Revelation was written, the church probably consisted mostly of a second and third generation of believers.

Jesus mentions many commendable things about this congregation at Ephesus. They were serving the Lord with great fervor and effort, and Jesus tells them, "I know your works, your labor, your patience, and that you cannot bear those who are evil" (Revelation 2:2). Jesus in no way criticized their works, their labor, or their patience.

> As we talk to our God and Father about you,
> we think of your faithful work, your loving deeds, and your
> continual anticipation of the return of our Lord Jesus Christ.
> 1 Thessalonians 1:3 NLT

Could the same thing be said of us? Does the Lord know of the work and labor we undertake for Him? Do you think He's aware of what we're doing?

The answer: God is aware of every little thing we do for Him.

Sometimes when we're serving the Lord, we may feel we're unappreciated. Perhaps no one thanks us or encourages us. They may not notice us.

But when we fail to get from other believers any attention or acclaim or affirmation about what we do for the Lord, know this: Jesus is saying,

BECAUSE

"I *have* noticed. I'm aware of it. I know your works, your labor, and your patience. I'm pleased with what you're doing."

That's why He tells us in Matthew 6:3–4, "But when you do a charitable deed, do not let your left hand know what your right hand is doing, that your charitable deed may be in secret; and your Father who sees in secret will Himself reward you openly." God sees.

The Lord's promise to His people...

If you give even a cup of cold water to one of the least of my followers, you will surely be rewarded.
JESUS, IN MATTHEW 10:42 NLT

With God in prayer...

Give thanks to the Lord for His promise to reward you and all believers for our faithfulness.

Because the Lord sees...

What encouragement do you need to offer today to those whom you see serving the Lord—even in "little things"?

Your own reflections... personal application... personal prayer points...

Wednesday

MAKING A DIFFERENCE

In the Book of Revelation, when Jesus gave His message to the church of Ephesus, He commended them for their discernment: "You have examined the claims of those who say they are apostles but are not. You have discovered they are liars" (Revelation 2:2 NLT).

This church also helped stop the spread of evil in their community. Jesus told them, "I know you don't tolerate evil people" (Revelation 2:2 NLT)

What a wonderful quality that was! How we need more discernment in our churches today. Far too many Christians are completely gullible, simply accepting anything anyone says in the name of the Lord. But the believers in the church of Ephesus were careful. They tested all things according to Scripture. (This biblical testing grid was also true from the beginning for the church in the city of Berea. In Acts 17:11 we read that when the apostle Paul and Silas first preached the gospel there, "they received the word with all readiness, and searched the Scriptures daily to find out whether these things were so.")

The Ephesian believers were faithful both to Scripture and to the Lord, and therefore Jesus could tell them, "You have persevered and have patience, and have labored for My name's sake and have not become weary" (Revelation 2:3). These believers were working hard and giving everything for the Lord. And it made a difference.

> We work hard and suffer much in order that people will believe the truth, for our hope is in the living God, who is the Savior of all people, and particularly of those who believe.
>
> 1 Timothy 4:10 NLT

Have you wondered what kind of a place your community would be if God hadn't raised up your church and others in the area? How many lives would still be messed up? How many marriages would be over? How many persons would have gone to hell?

This side of heaven, we'll never know the full impact our churches are having.

> The Lord's promise to His people...
>
> My chosen shall long enjoy the work of their hands.
> They shall not labor in vain.
> ISAIAH 65:22–23 ESV

With God in prayer...

·Give thanks to the Lord for the difference He has made in *your* community through your church. (And I trust you *are* a part of a strong healthy church. If not, remember: You need the church, and the church needs you!)

Because God works through His church...

When it comes to your own involvement and work in your church, what further commitment should you be considering?

Your own reflections... personal application... personal prayer points...

Thursday

NO SUBSTITUTE FOR LOVE

Although Jesus acknowledged many virtues in the church of Ephesus, He also had a major criticism: "You have left your first love" (Revelation 2:4). What does this mean?

It means these Ephesian believers were so busy maintaining their separation from evil and laboring in ministry that they were forgetting their adoration of Christ. They were forgetting that labor is no substitute for love.

I have this against you, that you have left your first love.

Jesus, in Revelation 2:4

Only fear the LORD, and serve Him in truth with all your heart; for consider what great things He has done for you.

1 Samuel 12:24

Is that also true for the church today? Have we left our first love? Sometimes the church gets involved in many political or social causes. But has our passion for that which is temporarily good displaced our passion for that which is *eternally* good? Is our *work* for Jesus overtaking our worship of Him?

But is it really such a big deal to leave your first love?

Let's look at it this way. Imagine your husband or wife walked up to you and said, "Honey, I want to tell you something. I no longer love you. But rest assured, everything is fine. I'll continue living with you. I'll continue being a parent to our children. I'll continue doing all the things a spouse and a parent should do. But I just don't love you anymore."

How would this hit you? Do you think this lack of love would impact

BECAUSE . . .

your relationship? Of course it would, because all you do for each other flows out of love.

This is what was happening with the church in Ephesus. And Jesus knows that when there's a weakening in our love for Him, it's only a matter of time before it will affect our actions.

The Lord's promise to His people...

Love never fails [never fades out or becomes obsolete or comes to an end].

1 CORINTHIANS 13:8 AMP

With God in prayer...

Honestly express your love for the Lord.

Because Christ is worthy of your best and highest love...

Honestly search your heart and life for any evidence of a weakening in your affection for Christ.

Your own reflections... personal application... personal prayer points...

Friday

IS THE HONEYMOON OVER?

Think again about the words of Jesus in Revelation 2:4—"I have this against you, that you have left your first love."

"First love" is similar to what two newlyweds experience. This kind of love is portrayed in an Old Testament passage where God says, "I remember you, the kindness of your youth, the love of your betrothal" (Jeremiah 2:2). God was saying to His people, "I remember when we had that honeymoon type of relationship." It was a close, intimate love.

> The Lord had a delight in loving your fathers, and He chose their descendants after them, you above all peoples, as it is this day.
> Deuteronomy 10:15 AMP

This isn't to say two married people should maintain forever that feeling of butterflies in their stomachs that they sensed when they first fell in love. I remember after I first met my wife, I would experience a loss of appetite and would get sort of jittery around her. Today, I'm more in love with her than I've ever been, but I'm not necessarily feeling those same emotions I felt when we first met.

In the same way, the Lord isn't saying He expects us to walk around with a constant emotional buzz in our lives as a result of being His followers. But He's speaking of a love that doesn't lose sight of the very things that brought it into being.

> In Christ Jesus, neither circumcision nor uncircumcision counts for anything, but only faith activated and energized and expressed and working through love.
> Galatians 5:6 AMP

When a husband and wife begin to take each other for granted, when their life begins to become a mere routine and the romance is dying, then they can know their marriage is in danger. This can also happen to us as believers in our relationship with the Lord. We can start taking Him for granted. We can start taking our church for granted. We can start taking our faith for granted.

Sure, we're still going through the motions, but have we left our first love?

> The Lord's promise to His people...
>
> There are three things that will endure—faith, hope, and love—and the greatest of these is love.
>
> 1 CORINTHIANS 13:13 NLT

With God in prayer...

Search your own heart and ask yourself this question: Have I left my first love?

Because Christ is worthy of your best and highest love ...

Search your heart and life: In any way, are you taking for granted your Lord, your church, or your faith?

Your own reflections... personal application... personal prayer points...

SIMPLICITY AND PURITY

There are two earmarks of a believer who's continuing to live in a first-love relationship with God—simplicity and purity.

Look closely at what the apostle Paul writes to the believers of his day about this: "I promised you as a pure bride to one husband, Christ. But I fear that somehow you will be led away from your *pure and simple devotion to Christ*" (2 Corinthians 11:2–3 NLT).

Are you living a simple and pure life as a believer today?

To be simple doesn't mean you're a simpleton or that you're naive. But we should never outgrow our sense of wonder and awe of who God is. We should never lose our childlike faith.

Yes, we should grow up and become mature men and women of God in our knowledge of Scripture and in our understanding of who God is. But we should always have a simple, childlike faith and dependence on God. In other words, we should live simple and pure lives.

Yet this is an area that's breaking down in the lives of many believers today. They begin to compromise morally. They begin to compromise ethically. They begin to compromise spiritually. There's a breakdown, and the purity is gone.

Don't let this happen.

> I am fearful...your minds may be corrupted and seduced from **wholehearted** and sincere and pure **devotion** to Christ.
>
> 2 Corinthians 11:3 AMP

There's a difference between someone who's in a first-love relationship with God and someone who's not. In a first-love relationship, our work for the Lord is a work of faith. But when our first love is lost, it's just work.

There's a big difference between being tired *in* the work of the Lord and being tired *of* the work of the Lord. When our love for Him is full, our service to Him comes easily. It's the overflow of a Christ-filled life.

> The Lord's promise to His people...
>
> Take my yoke upon you. Let me teach you, because I am humble and gentle, and you will find rest for your souls. For my yoke fits perfectly, and the burden I give you is light.
> JESUS, IN MATTHEW 11:29–30 NLT

With God in prayer...

Ask God to help you live a pure and simple life of loving devotion to Him.

Because Christ is worthy of your best and highest love ...

How evident right now are *purity* and *simplicity* in your relationship with Christ?

Your own reflections... personal application... personal prayer points...

WATCH OUT FOR HEART DISEASE

I once knew a guy who was always in the best shape. I would run into him a couple of times a year, and he always made a point of reminding me he was in much better shape than I was.

He would say to me, "Feel my arm!"

Reluctantly I would touch his bicep and reply, "It's hard."

"That's right!" he would say. But he was also a very stressed-out kind of guy. Very intense and high-strung.

One day, I received the terrible news that he'd died of a sudden heart attack. The news caught us all by surprise, and I was deeply saddened.

Physically, this guy had it all together on the outside. He was in great shape. But inside, his heart was in trouble.

You may have the outward appearance of having it all together spiritually. You may have incredible stamina and energy in the Lord's work. But what good is all that if you have heart disease?

Let not my **heart** be drawn to what is evil.

Psalm 141:4 NIV

You might be able to flex your spiritual muscles in front of other people. You might say, "Look at my schedule! Look at all I'm doing for God. Look at my accomplishments." That's good. Sort of.

When Jesus told the believers at Ephesus they'd left their first love (Revelation 2:4), He was getting to the heart of the matter, the root of success or failure in the Christian life. He was saying, "You're leaving this first love. You're neglecting these basic things."

BECAUSE . . .

You have **forgotten** Me and cast Me behind your back.

Ezekiel 23:35

That's when the Christian life becomes drudgery. That's when you start saying, "There are so many rules. There are so many restrictions. I want to live as I please. I want to be free." When you begin to think like this, you're leaving your first love.

> The Lord's promise to His people…
>
> If your heart turns away so that you do not hear,
> and are drawn away, and worship other gods and
> serve them, I announce to you today that you shall surely perish.
> DEUTERONOMY 30:17–18

With God in prayer…

Ask the Lord to help your heart to remain pure and passionate for Him.

Because Christ is worthy of your best and highest love …

Are there any traces of "heart disease" right now in your relationship with the Lord? Are your spiritual eyes open wide enough to see such traces?

Your own reflections… personal application… personal prayer points…

DESTINED FOR A FALL

Show me a believer who has fallen into any sin, whatever sin it may be, and I'll show you a believer who somewhere in time—maybe months ago, maybe years ago—left his or her first love.

Jesus told the believers at Ephesus to remember from where they'd fallen. We might dismiss this as a trivial issue. We might think, "Okay, so I'm not as close to the Lord as I used to be. Don't be too hard on me."

> Remember therefore from **where** you have fallen.
>
> Revelation 2:5

But it's of the greatest importance that we maintain our first-love relationship with Christ.

David stands as an example of this. We rightly remember him as the man after God's own heart and the sweet psalmist of Israel. He was. But we also remember him as a murderer and an adulterer.

We ask ourselves how someone who had risen as high spiritually as David had could fall so low morally? It's simple: He left his first love. That was at the root of it.

As a youth, David was often out in the wilderness, worshiping the Lord, playing on his stringed instrument, and singing his songs of praise to God. But after he became king, though he was a great ruler for a time, he didn't worship the Lord as he once had. Instead of maintaining vital spiritual activity, he became idle. It was only a matter of time until something led to his fall.

That's what many of us are like. We're setting ourselves up for a fall, because we're neglecting our passion and our devotion to Christ. Yet this passion and devotion are foundational.

How strong is your passion and **devotion** for Christ today?

BECAUSE...

265

Let's make sure we aren't leaving our first love.

> The Lord's promise to His people...
>
> Give thanks to the LORD Almighty, for the LORD is good.
> His faithful love endures forever!
> JEREMIAH 33:11 NLT

With God in prayer...

On this new day, honestly express again your love for the Lord.

Because Christ is worthy of your best and highest love ...

Have you in any way set yourself up for a fall because of any recent distancing from the Lord?

Your own reflections... personal application... personal prayer points...

Wednesday

REMEMBER

When Jesus found a fatal flaw in the church at Ephesus—that they were leaving their first love—He also gave His prescription for renewal and revival. They're the three R's of returning to our first love—*remember, repent,* and *repeat.*

First, you need to remember—and keep on remembering. What should you remember? You should remember where you were when Jesus Christ first found you. You were separated from Him by sin and on your way to a certain judgment. But He graciously and lovingly reached out to you and forgave you. All of us were separated from God and facing judgment. The essential thing Christ did for you is the same thing He did for every person.

> Remember therefore from where you have fallen;
> **repent** and do the first works...
> Revelation 2:5

David described it this way: "He also brought me up out of a horrible pit, out of the miry clay, and set my feet upon a rock, and established my steps. He has put a new song in my mouth—praise to our God" (Psalm 40:2–3). Every Christian can say this. That's what Christ did for us.

Second, you need to remember where you were at the highest point of your love for Jesus. When was that high point in your spiritual life? Was it a month ago? Was it a year ago? Was it ten years? Or is it today?

What has been the true high point in your **love** for Christ?

BECAUSE...

Can you say, "At this moment in my life, I believe I'm as close to the Lord as I've ever been." If you can say that, praise God. If not, remember when you were closest to the Lord, mark it in your mind, and make it your aim to return there once again.

> The Lord's promise to His people...
>
> I will heal their waywardness and love them freely,
> for my anger has turned away from them.
> HOSEA 14:4 NIV

With God in prayer...

On this new day, take some time to remember your brightest and best times with the Lord. If they're in your past and not your present, why not take steps to change that?

Because Christ is worthy of your best and highest love ...

Are you as close to Christ now as you have ever been? If not, what must you do?

Your own reflections... personal application... personal prayer points...

REPENT AND REPEAT

The word *repent* means to change your direction. This means if I realize I'm not living in a first-love relationship with the Lord as I ought to, I need to repent.

Make no mistake about it: Leaving your first love is a sin. Jesus said, "Remember therefore from where you have *fallen*" (Revelation 2:5). So this isn't just stumbling; this is being in a fallen state. Christ is telling us to repent and to get out of the state we're in.

Then Jesus tells them, "Repent and do the first works" (Revelation 2:5). This is key.

For example, maybe you know you need to get into better shape physically than you're in. You didn't necessarily aspire to be a pear, but that's the shape you find yourself in today. So, you decide to do something about it. What do you do?

First, you remember. You remember there was a time when you were in better shape. You remember how you exercised more often, and how you disciplined yourself in regard to your eating habits. So you decide to return to that old regimen. You remember. You repent. And you repeat.

Now let's apply that to the spiritual life. You remember there was a time when you were doing well spiritually. Your fire was burning brightly. Was there anything different you did then that you aren't doing now? If so, identify it and go back and do what you did before.

> Repent, and turn from all your transgressions,
> so that iniquity will not be your ruin.
> Ezekiel 18:30

BECAUSE

This is not rocket science here; it's 100% doable by the grace of God.

Return to your rest, O my soul, for the
LORD has dealt bountifully with you.

Psalm 116:7

That's what Jesus tells us to do. Remember. Repent. Repeat.

The Lord's promise to His people...

Let the people turn from their wicked deeds.
Let them banish from their minds the very thought
of doing wrong! Let them turn to the LORD that he may have
mercy on them. Yes, turn to our God, for he will abundantly pardon.

ISAIAH 55:7 NLT

With God in prayer...

On this new day, honestly express again to the Lord your love for Him.

Because Christ is worthy of your best and highest love ...

In your past, what has helped you most to stay close to the Lord in your
love for Him? What can you do today to repeat this?

Your own reflections... personal application... personal prayer points...

LOSING OUR LIGHT

When we come across the word *lampstand* in the book of Revelation, it's a symbol of the church and speaks of something that displays light. So when Jesus told the church of Ephesus that He would remove their lampstand from its place, He was telling them that in spite of the privilege they once had enjoyed in Ephesus, they were in danger of losing their light.

The church that has lost its love will soon lose its light.

In Revelation 2:4, the phrase "you have left your first love" could speak of both a love for God and a love for people. When you're truly loving God as you ought to, you'll have the love you need for people.

A church that has lost its love for the Lord and its love for people is a church that's losing its light, losing its effectiveness, and losing its testimony.

> I have this **complaint** against you.
> You don't love me or each other as you did at **first!**
> Revelation 2:4 NLT

One of the most powerful testimonies a church can have is when someone comes into their midst and senses a genuine love for other people and for God. If a church loses that, it will lose its testimony.

Today our nation is filled with cavernous church sanctuaries that once had a powerful impact on their communities as the Word of God was faithfully proclaimed. But the original leadership grew old. Their legacy was not successfully passed on. Unsound tendencies crept in, and now those churches have lost their light in the community.

It can happen anyplace. It can happen in an individual life as well.

God help us to always have a testimony and a life that truly makes a difference.

> The Lord's promise to His people...
>
> If we are living in the light of God's presence, just as Christ is, then we have fellowship with each other, and the blood of Jesus, his Son, cleanses us from every sin.
>
> 1 JOHN 1:7 NLT

With God in prayer...

What kind of testimony does your church have in your community? How active a role are you playing in your church? Ask the Lord to help you be an effective and committed church member.

Because Christ is worthy of your best and highest love ...

How is God leading and helping you in reaching out in genuine love for others?

Your own reflections... personal application... personal prayer points...

THREE QUALITIES OF A GODLY PERSON

At the very end of James 1, we find three tests that determine whether we're truly spiritual. If you're truly a godly person, these three things should characterize your life.

> If you claim to be religious but don't **control** your tongue, you are just fooling yourself, and your religion is worthless. Pure and lasting religion in the sight of God our Father means that we must **care** for orphans and widows in their troubles, and refuse to let the world corrupt us.
>
> James 1:26-27 NLT

One, *you'll control your tongue.* A true test of a person's spirituality is not the ability to speak one's mind but the ability to hold one's tongue. We may pride ourselves in the fact that we aren't immoral or violent. But we may inflict incalculable pain on someone by wounding them with our words and stealing their good name or reputation. So we need to control our tongues.

Two, *you'll care about those who are in need.* Jesus explained (in Matthew 25:34–40) that when we give sustenance to the hungry, or hospitality to strangers, or clothing to those who need it, or companionship to those who are sick or in prison, we're actually doing these things for and to *Him.* That's true spirituality.

> Do you know someone right **now** who could really use your help in a tangible way? Show them God's love by **helping** them.

Three, *you'll keep yourself uncorrupted by the world.* God is ultimately the One who keeps us uncorrupted, but we need to make sure we don't conform to the world and its standards. It's faith alone that justifies, but faith that justifies can never be alone. If your faith is real, there will be changes in your life as a result of it.

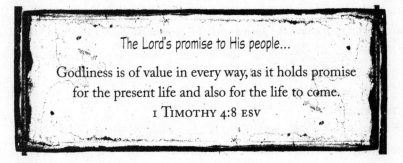

The Lord's promise to His people...

Godliness is of value in every way, as it holds promise
for the present life and also for the life to come.
1 TIMOTHY 4:8 ESV

With God in prayer...

Let the light of God's presence help you to examine your life in these three areas.

Because He wants you to be godly...

On a practical basis, what should you be doing in each of these three areas in the immediate future?

Your own reflections... personal application... personal prayer points...

PRIORITIES

After a heavy rainstorm, a man was out driving in the country when he came across an old farmer surveying the ruins of a collapsed barn. He pulled over and asked the farmer what happened.

"Roof fell in," the farmer replied.

"How did that happen?" asked the stranger.

"Too many leaks," the farmer said. "After all these years, it just finally rotted through."

"But—couldn't you have fixed the leaks before it came to this?"

"Well," the farmer answered, "when the weather was good, there wasn't a need for it. And when it rained, it was just too wet to work on."

Isn't it amazing that when you really *want* to do something, you find the time for it, no matter how busy you are? But when it comes to something you really don't want to do, it doesn't find room in your schedule, no matter how important it might be.

This can happen when it comes to our Christian life as well. If we're serving God only when it's convenient, we're settling for second-best. If we make time for the things of God only when something more appealing doesn't come along first, we're missing out on what God wants to do in our lives.

> Seek first the kingdom of God and His righteousness.
>
> Jesus, in Matthew 6:33

How much better it is to make time for the things of God—to put the things of God above everything else. How much better it is to get our priorities right.

So instead of making excuses, make time for the Lord. It's not only the simple way to live, but also the best way.

The Lord's promise to His people...

The LORD will give grace and glory; no good thing
will He withhold from those who walk uprightly.

PSALM 84:11

With God in prayer...

Evaluate with God your true priorities in life.

Because God's priorities are best...

In obedience to God, what do you need to make time for that you've
been delaying or neglecting? Get started on it today.

Your own reflections... personal application... personal prayer points...

Tuesday

SMALL OPENINGS INTO YOUR LIFE

When I was a kid, I collected snakes. I don't know why, but I thought snakes were cool. My goal in life was to be a herpetologist (an expert on reptiles). I read up on snakes and owned many of them over the years.

My mom, who was tolerant of my unusual hobby, took me to the pet store one day to pick up a new snake. Excitedly I loaded it in the trunk of the car in a little box, but by the time we got home, the box was empty. The snake was gone. There had been just a little opening in that box, and my new pet escaped.

My mom said, "I'm never driving that car again." But a situation arose in which she had to drive. As she was waiting at a traffic light, she felt a cold coil drop onto her ankle. She was certain the missing snake was making its reappearance, so she opened the car door and jumped out, screaming at the top of her lungs.

A police officer happened to be there and asked what was wrong. She told him a snake was in her car. He went over to investigate, and as it turned out, the "snake" she felt was actually a hose that had come loose and fallen down onto her leg.

We never found the snake. (The good news: I ended up with the car!)

> Put on the whole armor of God, that you may be able to stand against the wiles of the devil.
>
> Ephesians 6:11

The devil is like that snake. When you give him a small opening in your life, watch out. You may think, "I'll just compromise a little bit here. I'll just lower my guard a little bit there. I can handle it. This is no problem." But the next thing you know, the devil has sunk his fangs into you, and you're going down fast. So be careful.

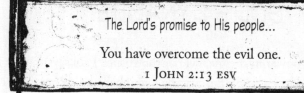

The Lord's promise to His people...

You have overcome the evil one.

1 JOHN 2:13 ESV

With God in prayer...

Remember again the pattern of prayer that Jesus taught us: "Do not lead us into temptation, but deliver us from the evil one" (Matthew 6:13).

Because Christ has already defeated Satan...

How can you be more bold and proactive in protecting yourself spiritually from enemy attacks?

Your own reflections... personal application... personal prayer points...

Wednesday

GOD'S DYNAMITE

There's explosive power in the message of the gospel. Paul says that "it is the power of God to salvation for everyone who believes" (Romans 1:16).

> This Good News about Christ...is the power of God at work, saving everyone who believes.
>
> Romans 1:16 NLT

The word for *power* that Paul used in this verse is from the Greek word *dunamis*. It's the same word Jesus used in Acts 1:8: "But when the Holy Spirit has come upon you, you will receive power [*dunamis*] and will tell people about me everywhere" (NLT). (The English words *dynamic, dynamo,* and *dynamite* are all descended from this Greek word *dunamis*.)

Paul was saying that the very message of the gospel is the dynamite of God. It's the dynamic of God.

We often underestimate the gospel's raw power to reach even the most hardened heart. Some of us may think we need to add to the gospel, or gloss it over, or even complicate it. But what we need to know is that there is distinct power in the simple message of the life, words, death, and resurrection of Jesus Christ.

So don't underestimate the gospel's appeal. Don't be ashamed of its simplicity. Don't add to it or take away from it. Just proclaim it, then stand back and watch what God will do.

As Paul said, "I know very well how foolish the message of the cross sounds to those who are on the road to destruction. But we who are being saved recognize this message as the very power of God" (1 Corinthians 1:18 NLT).

For Christ didn't send me to baptize, but to preach the Good News—and not with clever speeches and high-sounding ideas, for fear that the cross of Christ would lose its power.

1 Corinthians 1:17 NLT

The gospel is a simple message, one that we in the church have heard time and time again. But we should never underestimate its power.

The Lord's promise to His people...

Now let me remind you...of the Good News...for your faith is built on this wonderful message. And it is this Good News that saves you if you firmly believe it.

1 CORINTHIANS 15:1–2 NLT

With God in prayer...

Thank Him fully for what the gospel has done for you.

Because the gospel is God's dynamite...

With sure confidence in the gospel's power, who can you go to now and share with them this good news?

Your own reflections... personal application... personal prayer points...

TURNING TRIAL INTO TEMPTATION

If we aren't careful, testing on the outside can become temptation on the inside. When circumstances are difficult, we might find ourselves complaining against God, questioning His love, or resisting His will. At this point, Satan will provide an opportunity to escape the difficulty, and that opportunity becomes a temptation.

You'll go through hardships. You'll go through trials. When you do, you have a choice. You can turn to God in complete faith and humility and say, "Lord, I don't know what to do. I don't know what the answer is. I'm giving this situation to You." Or your testing can turn into a temptation, and you fall for it: You get angry with God or even rebel against Him.

It is written..."You shall not **tempt** the LORD your God."

Jesus, in Matthew 4:7

This is what happened to Abraham when he arrived in Canaan. A great famine came, and he wasn't able to care for his flocks and herds. Here was an opportunity to trust in God, but instead of learning from this trial, Abraham turned it into a temptation. The Bible says he went down to Egypt, and there—in order to preserve his life—he asked his wife Sarah to say she was his sister, because she was beautiful. God had to deal strongly with Abraham to bring him back to a place of obedience.

Temptation comes from the lure of our own evil desires. These evil desires lead to evil actions, and evil actions lead to **death**.

James 1:14-15 NLT

When we fall into temptation, let's not blame it on God. It's our own fault. To pray for strength to resist temptation, and then to rush into a place of vulnerability, is like putting your hands into a fire and praying you won't be burned. We bring it on ourselves.

> The Lord's promise to His people...
>
> God blesses the people who patiently endure testing.
> Afterward they will receive the crown of life that
> God has promised to those who love him.
> JAMES 1:12 NLT

With God in prayer...

Confess any tendencies you've had to blame God for your temptations, including the temptation to resist or complain about the trials He brings into your life.

Because God must sometimes deal strongly with you...

What exactly is the path of obedience God wants you to adhere closely to right now, and how is God helping you do that through His discipline?

Your own reflections... personal application... personal prayer points...

Friday

WHEN BELIEVERS STRAY

We all know people who once walked with the Lord, but have since thrown in the towel. They've abandoned the faith. They've gone back to their old life.

What can we do for them in these situations? Should we confront these people? Should we just leave them alone? Should we just forget about them?

James shows us the value of doing something about it:

My dear brothers and sisters, if anyone among you wanders away from the truth and is brought back again, you can be sure that the one who brings that person back will save that sinner from death and bring about the forgiveness of many sins. (James 5:19–20 NLT)

The apostle Paul gives us additional insight about this:

Dear brothers and sisters, if another Christian is overcome by some sin, you who are godly should gently and humbly help that person back onto the right path. And be careful not to fall into the same temptation yourself. (Galatians 6:1 NLT)

Notice the warning in that last sentence. *You have the potential to fall.* So do I.

You might tell yourself, "Not me! I've been walking with the Lord for twenty-seven years now." But there's always tomorrow.

One thing we need to recognize about ourselves is our vulnerability. Each of us can admit that we're "prone to wander," as an old hymn expresses it, "prone to leave the God I love." And the first step down this wandering path is our own self-confidence.

Keep a close **watch** on yourself and on your teaching. Stay true to
what is right, and God will **save** you and those who hear you.
1 Timothy 4:16 NLT

Therefore, if we see someone else who has strayed from the faith, we should restore such a person in the spirit of meekness. After all, one day it could be you or me who needs to be restored.

The Lord's promise to His people...

You have allowed me to suffer much hardship, but you will restore me to life again and lift me up from the depths of the earth.
PSALM 71:20 NLT

With God in prayer...

Give thanks for how the Lord has brought you back from your wanderings.

Because the Lord is our Restorer...

Who should you be helping now to come back from their spiritual wandering? How can you help restore them?

Your own reflections... personal application... personal prayer points...

OUTWARDLY ALIVE, INWARDLY DEAD

Have you ever seen something that looked quite charming at a distance, but as you got closer, you realized it wasn't what you thought?

This is how the church of Sardis could be described, in the message that Jesus gave to them in the Book of Revelation. Outwardly they did the right things, but inwardly, something was missing.

Historically, Sardis was an impressive looking city, built on a mountain rising fifteen hundred feet above a valley floor. The people of Sardis were confident their walls would be impossible to scale—so confident that they did not place enough guards outside to keep watch. Sardis as a city was characterized by complacency—and that complacency seemed to find its way into the church there as well.

The church of Sardis was essentially living in the past and resting on its laurels. To this church, Jesus said, "I know all the things you do" (Revelation 3:1 NLT). The Lord began with words of commendation for what good He found there. This was not a lazy or inactive church. They were well-known. Outwardly, they had every indication of a church on the move.

But inwardly, something was wrong that only Jesus could see: They were dead. "You have a reputation for being alive—but you are dead" (Revelation 3:1 NLT).

> Consider yourselves **dead** to sin and able to live for the glory of God through Christ Jesus.... Give yourselves **completely** to God since you have been given new life.
>
> Romans 6:11, 13 NLT

So Jesus told them, "Strengthen what little remains, for even what is left is at the point of death.... Go back to what you heard and believed at first; hold to it firmly and turn to me again" (Revelation 3:2–3 NLT).

Have you been in a state of spiritual deadness? Maybe you're doing all the right things outwardly, but inwardly, you know something isn't right. Remember Jesus' words to a spiritually deadened church.

The Lord's promise to His people...

And this is the promise that He has promised us—eternal life.
1 JOHN 2:25

With God in prayer...

Ask God to help you strengthen and deepen your obedience to Him today, and to show you how to do this.

Because Christ sees fully into your heart...

Is there spiritual deadness in you that needs shaking up? How can you "strengthen what little remains," and "go back to what you heard and believed at first," and "hold to it firmly" (Revelation 3:2–3 NLT)?

Your own reflections... personal application... personal prayer points...

THE REAL SOURCE OF THE PROBLEM

During a time when El Niño weather patterns were noticeably affecting Southern California, I witnessed an interesting phenomenon: It was the one thing on which people blamed practically everything. No matter what it was, El Niño was the culprit: "This has been a wet year." El Niño. "It's hot today." El Niño. "It's a little cooler than normal today." El Niño. "There's a crime wave going on." El Niño. "Why did that marriage fall apart?" El Niño. "Why were you late for work today?" El Niño.

Nowadays the story's often the same; just substitute "global warming" as the universal culprit.

It's convenient to have a scapegoat, especially when no one wants to take responsibility for their actions. We're living in a day when we love to blame someone or something for the things we do. (Of course, the problem is *never* us.) We find a million and one excuses to explain away our wrong behavior. It's so easy to blame someone else for our problems.

What are your most common excuses or scapegoats?

But what's really the source of our problems today? Is it low self-esteem? Is it tensions in our family? Is it the government? Is it our morally declining culture? Is it El Niño?

The Bible tells us the source of our problems: "What is causing the quarrels and fights among you? Isn't it the whole army of evil desires at war within you?" (James 4:1 NLT).

Our evil desires—that's exactly where these problems come from.

BECAUSE . . . .

Create in me a clean heart, O God.
Renew a right spirit within me.
Psalm 51:10 NLT

This is the answer to questions we may have about conflicts in our own lives and families and in our churches. It comes down to one simple thing: The problem is *us*. The problem is inside.

> The Lord's promise to His people...
>
> I will give you a new heart and put a new spirit within you.
> EZEKIEL 36:26

With God in prayer...

Talk with God about whatever evil desires are warring within you now. Yield these up to Him, and yield yourself to His control.

Because Christ is the full and complete answer to our greatest need...

Before God, are you being honest with yourself about how you view and seek to satisfy your true needs and desires?

Your own reflections... personal application... personal prayer points...

Tuesday

A MAN OF SORROWS

If I had the opportunity to know my entire future from today on, I think I would pass. Personally I would rather *not* know. (What about you?)

But Jesus, as He agonized in the Garden of Gethsemane, knew that in just a few short hours, He would be nailed to a Roman cross and crucified. He knew He would be humiliated. He knew He would be beaten and would experience a horrendous lashing. He knew the great anguish He was facing.

> Jesus brought them to an olive grove called Gethsemane; and he said, "Sit here while I go on ahead to pray"... and he began to be filled with anguish and deep distress.
>
> Matthew 26:36-37 NLT

It would be a horrendously difficult time, and He would experience deep loneliness and abandonment by His friends. Yet He went through it.

The Bible tells us Jesus was "a man of sorrows, acquainted with bitterest grief" (Isaiah 53:3 NLT). The Bible also says this about Him:

> This High Priest of ours understands our weaknesses, for he faced all of the same temptations we do, yet he did not sin. So let us come boldly to the throne of our gracious God. There we will receive his mercy, and we will find grace to help us when we need it. (Hebrews 4:15–16 NLT)

Did you catch that? Jesus *understands our weaknesses.* He has faced every temptation you and I have ever faced. He knows what you're going through. Your High Priest—that is, Jesus—has faced the challenges you presently face.

288

BECAUSE . . .

The next time you face difficulty, the next time you face hardship, the next time you feel misunderstood and abandoned, remember that Jesus already has experienced those things. You have Someone who understands you, sympathizes with you, and is there to strengthen you.

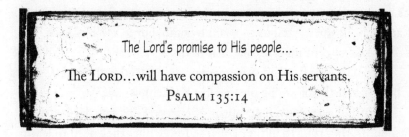

The Lord's promise to His people...

The LORD...will have compassion on His servants.
PSALM 135:14

With God in prayer...

·Share your sorrows and sufferings with the Lord, as you thank Him for how fully He understands.

Because Jesus was a Man of Sorrows...

Think of those around you who are dealing with sorrow and suffering. In Christ's name, go and be a comfort to them.

Your own reflections... personal application... personal prayer points...

Wednesday

THE INSIDE TRACK

It's no coincidence that Scripture uses the phrase "walk by faith." Notice that the Bible doesn't tell us to *sprint* by faith, but to *walk* by faith. To walk speaks of continual, regulated motion.

The Bible says Enoch was someone who walked with God (Genesis 5:22–24), and therefore "he pleased God" (Hebrews 11:5).

Many believers have their bursts of energy. For a few days or weeks or months, they run. Then they collapse for awhile. They need to learn what it is to walk with God.

Of course, in our fast-paced world we like things fast. We have microwave dinners, cell phones, instant messaging. We have so much technology to make our lives a little easier and, most importantly, faster. Then we come to the Christian life and we say, "All right, where's the shortcut?"

But there's no shortcut. "We *walk* by faith" (2 Corinthians 5:7), and it's a day-by-day process.

> For we walk by **faith**, not by sight.
> 2 Corinthians 5:7

However, although there's no shortcut, there *is* an angle; there *is* an inside track. It's very simple. The Bible declares that "the just shall live by faith" (Romans 1:17). Not by feeling. Not by emotion. Not by fear. Not by worries. *By faith.*

I know sometimes it seems like nothing's happening in our spiritual growth. We don't *feel* we're changing; we look at ourselves every day and don't necessarily observe any changes. But as we're walking by faith day by day, month by month, year by year, we *are* being transformed.

As you therefore have **received** Christ Jesus the Lord,
so walk in Him, rooted and built up in Him and established in the faith,
as you have been taught, abounding in it with **thanksgiving.**

Colossians 2:6-7

That's it. The just shall live by faith.

The Lord's promise to His people...

If your faith remains strong after being tried by fiery trials,
it will bring you much praise and glory and honor on the day
when Jesus Christ is revealed to the whole world.

1 PETER 1:7 NLT

With God in prayer...

Confess your faith in the Lord. Tell Him all that you *know* is true about
Him and about eternity.

Because we walk by faith...

How has God already transformed you? Give Him thanks for this.

Your own reflections... personal application... personal prayer points...

WANTED: NEW BELIEVERS

I love new believers. They're the lifeblood of the church.

When I have the privilege of speaking to other pastors, I tell them that if they don't have a constant flow of new believers coming into their congregations, they'll become spiritually dead. We can either evangelize or fossilize.

Show me a church in which new believers are not coming in, and I'll show you a church that's stagnating. Show me a church with new believers coming in on a regular basis, and I'll show you a church with vibrancy and life.

And the Lord added to the church daily those who were being saved.

Acts 2:47

Granted, new believers need older believers to stabilize them. New believers' hearts are full of zeal, but they don't always understand the ground rules. They need older believers to teach and guide them. Still, older believers also need new believers. They need their zeal. They need their passion. They need their excitement to remind them of what they've forgotten.

Sadly, it's usually the new believers who want to do the most when they know the least. In our church, when we ask people to help out with something, so often we have new believers come and say they want to help: "I'll do whatever you need." They decide they want to sign up to help in six ministries. While we're appreciative of their willingness to serve, we want them to have a good foundation first so they can be properly trained and equipped to do what God has called them to do.

On the other hand, there are older believers who have known the

Lord for years, maybe even decades, who don't give a passing thought to helping out at church. It should be just the opposite.

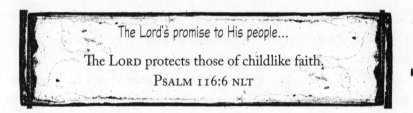

The Lord's promise to His people...

The LORD protects those of childlike faith.

PSALM 116:6 NLT

With God in prayer...

Ask God to renew in your heart the sense of zeal and passion that you may have experienced as a new believer.

Because of the excitement of new life...

Does your church include a healthy number of new believers? If not, how can this be changed?

Your own reflections... personal application... personal prayer points...

NEVER ALONE

Time and time again God reminded Paul of His presence with him, no doubt when he needed it the most.

He knew when Paul could use extra assurance. When Paul was in a prison cell in Jerusalem, the Lord came and "stood by him" and told him to be courageous (Acts 23:11). When Paul faced shipwreck in a storm, the Lord sent an angel to give reassurance to Paul and all those who were with him (Acts 27:23–24). Later, writing from a prison cell in Rome, Paul wrote of yet another time when "the Lord stood with me and gave me strength" (2 Timothy 4:17 NLT).

> For last night an angel of the God to whom I belong and whom I serve stood beside me, and he said, "Don't be afraid, Paul.... God in his goodness has granted safety to everyone sailing with you.
>
> Acts 27:23-24 NLT

In special ways, God reassured Paul of His presence.

God knows what we need, too, and He knows *when* we need it. You can take heart in the face of danger or uncertainty because of your awareness of God's presence with you. When your heart sinks, when it seems as though your life is falling apart, remember that the Lord is there with you. You aren't alone.

> I am with you always.
> Jesus, in Matthew 28:20

BECAUSE . . .

No, there aren't always easy answers. But we can be sure of this: He'll be with us through the storm.

God was standing by Paul's side, and God is with us in our storms as well. He may not necessarily send us an angel. We may not necessarily hear an audible voice. But if we pay attention, we can hear the still, small voice of God. And certainly, He'll speak to us through His Word.

> Now may the Lord of peace Himself give you peace always in every way. The Lord be with you all.
>
> 2 Thessalonians 3:16

Then we, like Paul, can reassure others that the Lord is in control.

The Lord's promise to His people...

My sheep hear My voice.
JESUS, IN JOHN 10:27

With God in prayer...

Be aware of the Lord's presence, and thank Him for it.

Because God is near...

What can you do to be more fully aware of the Lord's presence?

Your own reflections... personal application... personal prayer points...

SEIZING OPPORTUNITIES

One of the things that amazes me about the apostle Paul is how he always seemed to rise to the top of every situation and seized every opportunity to preach the gospel.

We read in the book of Acts that when Paul and Silas were thrown in prison, they began to sing praises to God at midnight. An earthquake struck, the walls fell, and the next thing you know, the very jailer who was responsible for chaining them up and whipping them asked, "What must I do to be saved?"

Later, when Paul was brought before the various dignitaries of Rome, he took advantage of every situation. For example, when he was before the governor Felix, he "reasoned" with this man "about righteousness, self-control, and the judgment to come" (Acts 24:25).

When he later stood before the governor Festus and King Agrippa, he asked them, "Why is it thought incredible by you that God raises the dead?" (Acts 26:8). Later Paul turned to the king and boldly asked, "Do you believe the prophets? I know that you do believe" (Acts 26:27).

In a voyage described in Acts 27, Paul was a prisoner on a ship. But when a long, terrifying storm struck them, it wasn't long before Paul was telling them how to save their lives—thanks to his faith in God—and everyone was listening to him!

The Lord will **deliver** me from every evil work and preserve me for His heavenly kingdom. To Him be **glory** forever and ever. Amen!

2 Timothy 4:18

Paul was bold. He didn't seem to be afraid of anything. He never seemed to get down, though he did at times.

The LORD is my light and my salvation; whom shall I fear?
The LORD is the strength of my life; of whom shall I be afraid?

Psalm 27:1-2

BECAUSE . . .

297

Paul's life wasn't always easy; in fact, it was extremely difficult. But the words he penned to the believers at Philippi seemed to always hold true: "I have learned in whatever state I am, to be content" (Philippians 4:11). He was fully convinced of the faithfulness of God and was sustained by that conviction.

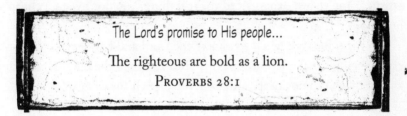

The Lord's promise to His people...

The righteous are bold as a lion.

PROVERBS 28:1

With God in prayer...

Tell God today all about your trust and contentment in Him, and about how convinced you are of His faithfulness.

Because the Lord will faithfully guard you...

How can you demonstrate more boldness in your witness for the Lord?

Your own reflections... personal application... personal prayer points...

THE REAL THING

Imagine you've just come out of a wonderful restaurant and had a great meal. You're thinking, "That was great."

Then you happen to glance over at the gutter and notice a discarded, half-eaten burrito from a fast-food restaurant. Are you going to say, "All right! A burrito!" and pick it up?

Of course not. You won't eat it, or even pick it up, because you're satisfied. You've just experienced the real thing. You don't want a cheap imitation.

In the same way, when you know the Lord and have been experiencing a real relationship with Him and then the devil comes along and offers you some cheap imitation, you'll see it for what it is.

When you see who Jesus is, then you see what the world is.

But if you're looking only at this world and not spending enough time with the Lord, you'll have a diminished view of God and an exalted view of this world—when it should be the other way around.

None of these things move me; nor do I count my life dear to myself, so that I may finish my race with joy, and the ministry which I received from the Lord Jesus, to testify to the gospel of the grace of God.

Acts 20:24

Everything you need in life is found in a relationship with God. You can discover this the easy way or the hard way.

Are you finishing your race with joy?

Or are you going outside your relationship with the Lord, trying to find some happiness that this world might offer?

I can tell you right now that trying to find happiness in what this world offers will be a dead-end street.

298

BECAUSE

What this world offers will never satisfy you, because once you've had the real thing, cheap imitations will never suffice.

> The Lord's promise to His people...
>
> I am the way, the truth, and the life.
> JESUS, IN JOHN 14:6

With God in prayer...

Pray for the people you know who are settling for only cheap imitations of life-fulfillment, instead of coming to Christ for the real thing.

Because Christ is the real thing...

Are you running your race with joy?

Your own reflections... personal application... personal prayer points...

Tuesday

DEALING WITH DISCOURAGEMENT

It isn't unusual for even the most spiritual people to have their days of doubt.

Moses, on one occasion at least, was overwhelmed by his circumstances. After he'd listened to the constant complaining of the children of Israel, he basically told the Lord, "I'm fed up. Just kill me. I don't want to deal with this another day" (see Numbers 11:15).

Elijah, after his contest with the prophets of Baal on Mt. Carmel, heard that Jezebel had put a contract out on his life. He was so overwhelmed by his circumstances, so discouraged, so uncertain, and so filled with doubt, that he too asked God to take his life (see 1 Kings 19:4).

> Why are you cast down, O my soul? And why are you **disquieted** within me? Hope in God; for I shall yet praise Him, the help of my **countenance** and my God.
>
> Psalm 42:11

Jeremiah, the great prophet, faced overwhelming discouragement. He was ridiculed and harassed for speaking the Word of God. Because he was tired of the pressure he was facing, it made him want to stop giving out God's Word altogether. He said, "The word of the Lord was made to me a reproach and a derision daily. Then I said, 'I will not make mention of Him, nor speak anymore in His name'" (Jeremiah 20:8–9).

In what circumstances are you most likely to get **discouraged?**

Even the great apostle Paul had moments when he was discouraged. He wrote to the church at Corinth, "We were burdened beyond measure, above strength, so that we despaired even of life" (2 Corinthians 1:8).

You aren't the only one who has ever faced doubt or uncertainty or been perplexed about why God didn't work in a certain way. But be assured that this is only because we can't see the big picture as He can.

The Lord's promise to His people...

God is our refuge and strength, a very present help in trouble.
PSALM 46:1

With God in prayer...

Pour out before your Father in heaven any sense of discouragement that you have been experiencing recently.

Because God is our refuge and strength...

Even if you aren't experiencing any discouragement now, what can you do to better prepare yourself for a time in the future when you may be battling it?

Your own reflections... personal application... personal prayer points...

Wednesday

TIME WELL SPENT

I heard the other day that the average American will have spent fifteen years in front of the television during his or her lifetime. Can you imagine fifteen years of sitting in front of that box, clicking away? What a waste of life.

On the other hand, the Bible speaks of many rewards in heaven for the person who faithfully serves the Lord during his or her lifetime, and even speaks of crowns that will be given. In fact, I think we might be shocked when the awards are presented in heaven. We may expect them to go to all the big names we know. But just imagine if most of the awards were given to someone named Maude Firkenbinder. You hadn't heard about her. She never pastored a church. She never recorded Christian music. She never wrote a book. But she used the gifts God gave her. Maybe God called her to be a person of prayer. Maybe she labored in obscurity somewhere. But God saw her faithfulness and rewarded her openly.

> Those who are **wise** shall shine like the brightness
> of the sky above; and those who turn many to
> **righteousness**, like the stars forever and ever.
>
> Daniel 12:3 ESV

When you get to heaven, what will you have to show for your life on this earth?

All your accomplishments will be evaluated when you stand before Christ. It will happen for every man; it will happen for every woman. It isn't so much a judgment for sin, but a judgment against time that was spent in a worthless way.

BECAUSE

Rejoice, O young man, in your youth, and let your heart cheer you in the days of your youth; walk in the ways of your heart, and in the sight of your eyes; but know that for all these God will bring you into judgment.

Ecclesiastes 11:9 303

Did you have more passion or excitement for your career or for a sport or for your possessions than you had for the things of God? It will all come to nothing. Wasted hours. Wasted days. Wasted years.

The Lord's promise to His people...

We must all stand before Christ to be judged. We will each receive whatever we deserve for the good or evil we have done in our bodies.

2 CORINTHIANS 5:10 NLT

With God in prayer...

Praise God that when He administers rewards and punishment in heaven, there will be nothing He fails to see from our lives on earth.

Because your life soon will end...

When you get to heaven, what will you have to show for your life on this earth?

Your own reflections... personal application... personal prayer points...

Thursday

IS THERE A CATFISH IN YOUR TANK?

I heard a story about some fish suppliers who were having problems shipping codfish from the East Coast. By the time it reached the West, it was spoiled. They froze it, but by the time it arrived, it was mushy. So, they decided to send it alive. But it arrived dead. They tried sending it alive again, but with one difference: They included a catfish in each tank. You see, the catfish is the natural enemy of the codfish. By the time the codfish arrived, they were alive and well, because they'd spent their entire trip actively fleeing the catfish.

Maybe God has put a catfish in your tank to keep you alive and well spiritually. It's called *persecution.* Maybe there's a person where you work who always has mocking questions for you every Monday morning regarding spiritual things. Maybe it's that neighbor who's giving you a hard time for your faith in Jesus. Maybe it's an unbelieving spouse or family member who resents your faith. You're wondering why this is happening.

Well, it's like that catfish. It's keeping you on your toes.

> Do not marvel, my brethren, if the world **hates** you.
> 1 John 3:13

Shortly before His crucifixion, Jesus told the disciples, "If you were of the world, the world would love its own. Yet because you are not of the world, but I chose you out of the world, therefore the world hates you" (John 15:19).

God will allow persecution in the life of the believer. If you're experiencing persecution, here are two things to remember:

1. Persecution confirms that you're a child of God.
2. Persecution causes you to cling closer to Jesus.

Blessed are you when men hate you, and when they exclude you, and
revile you, and cast out your name as evil, for the Son of Man's sake.
Rejoice in that day and leap for joy! For indeed your reward is
great in heaven, for in like manner their fathers did to the prophets. 305

Jesus, in Luke 6:22-23

When you're suffering persecution for your faith, remember: This
world is not your home.

> The Lord's promise to His people...
>
> In the world you will have tribulation; but be of good cheer,
> I have overcome the world.
> JESUS, IN JOHN 16:33

With God in prayer...

Thank God for all that He does to help keep you spiritually healthy.

Because God allows us to be persecuted...

What's the closest thing to a "catfish" in your life right now? How is God
using it to help you?

Your own reflections... personal application... personal prayer points...

Friday

THE ULTIMATE SIGN

Would miracles make more people believe? Would unbelievers become believers if they were to see a bona fide miracle?

> Then some of the scribes and Pharisees answered,
> saying, "Teacher, we want to see a sign from You."
> Matthew 12:38

In the Gospels, when the scribes and Pharisees wanted Jesus to show them a sign from God, it prompted Him to give them some of His most solemn and searching words:

> An evil and adulterous generation seeks after a sign, and no sign
> will be given to it except the sign of the prophet Jonah.... The
> men of Nineveh will rise in the judgment with this generation
> and condemn it, because they repented at the preaching of Jonah;
> and indeed a greater than Jonah is here. (Matthew 12:39, 41)

Jesus' response seems almost harsh. After all, here were some individuals who were simply asking for a miracle. He'd performed plenty of them; why not one more? Perhaps that miracle could have brought them to faith. Why didn't He grant their request?

The answer is that Jesus always looks at the motives behind what people say and do. He's far more interested in what's going on in our hearts than in what's coming out of our mouths. As He looked in their hearts, no doubt He saw the real reason behind their request: They wanted to destroy Jesus. Matthew 12:14 tells us that the Pharisees "went out and plotted against Him, how they might destroy Him."

Jesus died on the cross for them and for all of humanity, and rose again from the dead—all because we were all separated from God by sin. That's the message Jesus essentially was giving to the Pharisees. That's the message He essentially is giving to us.

Let the dead bury their own dead,
but you go and preach the kingdom of God.

Jesus, in Luke 9:60

It's the greatest sign of all. It's the *ultimate* sign.

> The Lord's promise to His people...
>
> He personally carried away our sins in his own body on the cross so we can be dead to sin and live for what is right. You have been healed by his wounds!
>
> 1 PETER 2:24 NLT

With God in prayer...

Give plenty of thanksgiving to the Lord for His ultimate sign, His death on the cross followed by His resurrection from the dead. Concentrate on all that this means for you.

Because He looks at our motives...

What miracles from God do you want to ask for, in integrity and truth, in your own life or in the lives of those around you?

Your own reflections... personal application... personal prayer points...

FROM ORDINARY TO EXTRAORDINARY

When Dwight L. Moody was a young man and not yet a world-famous evangelist, someone told him that the world has yet to see what God can do with and through the man who's totally committed to Him.

Those words went deep into young Dwight's heart, and he prayed, "Lord, I want to be that man." God did indeed lead Moody into an incredibly fruitful and famous ministry. In his lifetime, he reached millions with the gospel.

The book of Acts is a story of ordinary men and women—much like D. L. Moody—who did extraordinary things because they allowed God to have His way in their lives. In the same way, God wants to use you to turn your world upside down for Christ.

It starts with your saying, "Lord, I want to make a difference. I don't want this world to turn me around; I want to turn it around. Use me."

The world has yet to see what God can do with and through a man or woman totally committed to Him. Will God find such people today?

Can you say, as Moody did, "I want to be that person"?

> The eyes of the LORD search the whole earth in order to strengthen those whose hearts are fully committed to him.
>
> 2 Chronicles 16:9 NLT

If so, your life can make an exciting difference, as you see what God can do through you. But you must first be fully available to Him.

One of these days, your life will come to an end. What will you conclude about your life? How satisfying it will be to say, as Paul did, "I have fought a good fight, I have finished the race, and I have remained faithful" (2 Timothy 4:7 NLT).

On that day, what will you say?

BECAUSE . . .

> The Lord's promise to His people...
>
> Mark the blameless man, and observe the upright;
> for the future of that man is peace.
>
> PSALM 37:37

With God in prayer...

Tell the Lord honestly about your desire to make a difference in your world, and your desire to have Him use you.

Because your life will soon end...

At the end of your days on earth, how do you expect to feel about what you have done with your life?

Your own reflections... personal application... personal prayer points...

TOPIC INDEX

SCRIPTURE INDEX